BRF Book Club

The Well is Deep

R. R. Williams

The Well is Deep

Aspects of the Biblical Heritage

by R. R. Williams DD

Bishop of Leicester (1953–1978)

The Bible Reading Fellowship

First Published 1978

© BRF 1978

BRF Book Club no. 1

The Bible Reading Fellowship

BRF encourages regular informed Bible-reading as a means of renewal in the churches.

BRF publishes daily readings with explanatory notes:

Series A for adult readers with some knowledge of Scripture;

Series B brief notes, with Bible passages printed out;

Compass readings and work-book, for children;

Discovery for young adults and beginners.

BRF also publishes introductory booklets on Bible-reading, group study guides, children's aids, audio-visual material, etc.

BRF St Michael's House, 2 Elizabeth St, London SW1W 9RQ

BRF PO Box M, Winter Park, Florida 32790, USA

BRF Jamieson House, Constitution Ave, Reid ACT 2601, Australia

design/print Eyre & Spottiswoode Ltd

General Introduction

'My son, there is something else to watch out for. There is no end to the writing of books, and too much study will wear you out' (Ecclesiastes 12:12). No doubt, the preacher was speculating upon the barrenness of a great deal of his thinking and, as he indicates in the next verse, felt that, if only God was given his rightful place in life, all would fall into place. On the face of it, however, he seems to be suggesting a moratorium on publication! When one considers that volumes upon volumes have been written on the Bible, the question may well arise why the Bible Reading Fellowship should contemplate starting a Book Club, in which the books would actually deal with the Bible. The only justification can be the deep-seated conviction that there is still more to be found in the pages of Scripture – that it is no mere collection of sagas or historical documents, no mere survival from the religious aspirations of near-eastern peoples of a past age. If it were, the Bible would belong to a limited number of scholars interested in ancient literature or antiquities. As it is, this Book Club has been launched in the conviction that the Bible is no dead book, that its message is alive and communicates with contemporary man and contemporary society.

What is more, we can discover the Bible speaking a word of God to us, witnessing to that element of mystery in life, which enables us to break out of the prison of our own thinking and frantic attempts to save ourselves and our world. It speaks of life with a vision, life in response to a calling. It speaks of a God who makes his demands upon us and yet succours us and gives us direction for life. A word from God for us? More, still! For Christians this word finds its focus in the living word, Jesus Christ. For he is discovered as the way to life itself, for he encounters us as 'the way, the truth and the life' (John 14:6).

In his epilogue to the third and final volume of the Cambridge History of the Bible the late Professor Greenslade closed his remarks with reference to 'the Gospel which the

Bible perpetually proclaims'. He sees here the reason why, at the coronation of the British monarch, the Bible, when presented to the newly-crowned ruler, can be described as 'the most valuable thing that this world affords'. It was for this reason that Samuel Taylor Coleridge was able to exclaim, 'I do not find the Bible, the Bible finds me'.

Accordingly, the series of books in this new Book Club will indicate that the Bible is much more than a mine from which we may dig up an occasional ingot. The 'gospel' or 'good news' it proclaims impinges on every department of thought and action. The Bible can be misused as well as used. It can become a fetish and be detached from the actualities of human life. If, however, we consider the ways in which the Bible has been, is and can be used, we cannot fail to catch something of its continuing appeal and continuing relevance for today's world.

In *The Well is Deep* Bishop Williams is, first and foremost, giving his personal testimony to the impact of the Bible on his own life. There are depths within the Scriptures to be sounded and drawn upon. We are reminded first of the literary heritage we have in the English Bible and then of the truth that man's life belongs to real historical situations and is no vacuum existence. So the Bible is seen as presenting the trial and development of faith in the context of history. The Psalms next are looked at chiefly in terms of personal piety and devotion – with clock and calendar spelling out the totality of God's dealings with us. 'Memories of our Lord' focusses on Jesus himself, the way in which his life, death and resurrection were understood and how the faith in him was communicated. Doctrinal development in the Scriptures is seen as indicating both a basic unity of approach and yet the diversity of interpretation, which the individual and particularist character of experience necessitates. Finally, we are invited to see life moving out from the boundedness of everyday existence to partake of God's own immortality, as he raises us up from all that speaks of deadness and unfulfilment. The reader is asked to join the author in drawing upon the well! The additional study material seeks to present ways in which the waters of that well may be tested, but readers will want to pursue still further their own investigations.

R. J. HAMMER

Ronald Ralph Williams

Born in 1906, the son of a priest, Bishop Williams had an outstanding undergraduate career at Cambridge, studying first English (a love he has retained) and then Theology. He taught briefly at St Aidan's College, Birkenhead, prior to his ordination to a curacy in the Chelmsford Diocese. He returned to Ridley Hall as Chaplain in 1931, leaving there for the Church Missionary Society, where he served from 1934 to 1940 as Education Secretary. The war years he spent in the Religious Division of the Ministry of Information. In 1945 he returned to the sphere of education as Principal of St John's College, Durham and Lecturer in Theology for the University of Durham. He remained there until his consecration as Bishop of Leicester in 1953. He will have completed 25 years as Bishop when he retires at the end of 1978.

His academic links have been many – Visitor to Ridley Hall, Cambridge, an Honorary Fellow of St Peter's College, Oxford, one-time President of the Queen's College at Birmingham (1960–3) and also a Governor of St Augustine's College, Canterbury. He holds the Honorary DD of Cambridge and a similar LLD of Leicester. He served for many years as Chairman of the Church of England's Board of Social Responsibility and of the Commission for Relations with the Evangelical Church in Germany and also the Lutheran World Federation.

His interest in the Bible, as readers of this book will ascertain for themselves, has been maintained throughout his life and a series of commentaries and other books amply testify to his exegetical ability. He has always been a zealous participant in the conferences of the Studiorum Novi Testamenti Societas. His links with the Bible Reading Fellowship go back to pre-war days and he has served as a Council member continuously from 1946, becoming its Vice-Chairman in 1954 and Chairman in 1956.

R. J. H.

Contents

Preface

1. Deep Literary Appeal **1**

2. Deep Mines of History **9**

3. Deep Personal Piety **21**

4. Deep Memories of the Lord **33**

5. Deep Reflections on the Faith **43**

6. Deep Longings for Life Eternal **53**

7. Drawing from the Well **66**

Study Projects **73**

Preface

The title of this small book is ruthlessly torn from its context in the story of the encounter of Jesus with 'the woman at the well'. When she is offered living water by our Lord, she points out that 'the well is deep', and that he has nothing to draw with. I have used her words and applied them to the Bible. Here indeed is a deep well, full of information and inspiration, of comfort and challenge, of judgement and mercy. Every generation of Christian people has found 'something to draw with', but in the last resort everybody has to find what helps him most to draw up the 'living water' for the refreshment and strengthening of his own soul by this particular means of grace.

The Bible has been my constant companion for more than half a century of adult life, and the source and substance of my preaching ministry. In suggesting six ways in which 'the well is deep' I have not been explicitly autobiographical, except here and there, but in what I have tried to share with others here, I have doubtless revealed some of the vessels which I have found serviceable in drawing up 'living water' from the Scriptures. I hope that there may be some who are glad to share my interest and discoveries.

I am grateful to Mrs Gillian England for typing yet another manuscript, and to the staff of the Bible Reading Fellowship for providing the notes and study material.

I should like to dedicate this book to the Bible Reading Fellowship, whose Council I have been privileged to chair for many years.

Bishop's Lodge,   RONALD LEICESTER
Leicester
April 1978

1: Deep Literary Appeal

Thirty or forty years ago there was something of a fashion among publishers to issue well-produced volumes with some such title as 'The Bible as Literature'.[1] I distinctly remember, as a young clergyman, sharing the feelings of many a would-be Christian that we were witnessing some kind of an act of profanation. Naturally we knew that the Bible *was* literature; it was indeed a whole series of literatures. But to concentrate so entirely on the literary quality of the material, when we believed that the principal purpose of the Bible was to be a vehicle for the message of God, a channel for the life of Christ, was in some way inappropriate.

If we take the matter calmly, we may feel that we can go too far in ignoring the literary basis of the biblical revelation. There was a time in the Reformation controversies when it was held by some that to deny the continuing presence of Bread and Wine in the consecrated sacrament was to 'overthrow the nature of a sacrament'. Perhaps the same thing is relevant to the Scriptures. There is much more than literature to the Bible, but the basic vehicle is literature. Words, words, words – these are the materials which Christians believe God has used as channels for his grace and carriers of his divine glory.

We must distinguish at once between biblical literature in its original and its translated form. From the strictly historical point of view the Hebrew Scriptures (forgetting for the moment the short Aramaic[2] portions of the Old Testament) represent an important monument to history, thought, and feeling as they embodied themselves in the life and folk-history of an obscure semitic people based on the southern end of the Eastern Mediterranean. The writings can be dated from roughly 1000 BC to 165 BC. Some of them were written to be read, others were records of words originally intended for *spoken* use, like the speeches of the prophets. Others again

1

were written to be sung, of which the Psalms are an obvious example. This Hebrew literature can be placed alongside the other great literary families, for example those of the Greeks and the Latins.

When Christians speak of 'the Bible' they include not only the Hebrew Scriptures, which they call 'the Old Testament', but also the Christian writings, which are in Greek, and which they call 'the New Testament'. Considered by itself, as a literary phenomenon, precipitated by history, this is quite a separate 'literature'. Not only is its language different, but so is its date (roughly AD 50–100), and also its *provenance*. Its milieu was the Hellenistic Roman Empire of the eastern Mediterranean. It spread from Jerusalem to Rome.

In some Bible translations we find between the Old and New Testaments the Apocryphal writings.[3] These books were mostly written in either Hebrew or Aramaic, but survive in the Greek language (apart from 2 Esdras which has been preserved in a Latin translation). The books were popular among the Jewish *diaspora*, those Jews who were scattered throughout the eastern Mediterranean and especially in Alexandria, where the Greek version of the Old Testament was first issued. The Apocrypha formed part of this translation (although some of the additions date towards the end of the first century AD), but its books were excluded from the Hebrew Canon of the Old Testament.

These familiar facts are summarised here lest anyone should imagine that 'the Bible as Literature' can be fully described in terms of any English translation, but it is a fact that until relatively modern times it was the Authorised Version (1611)[4] that was principally in mind in the English-speaking world. Misunderstandings can so easily arise that even in the realm of translation some ground-clearing operations may be necessary.

To the casual observer the years from 1611 to the present day were completely dominated by the Authorised (King James) Version and, after examination, this is largely true. The examination is, however, very necessary. To begin with the Authorised Version itself was only the last (even if that) of a whole spate of translations running from Wycliffe in the

2

fourteenth century, through Tyndale, Coverdale and the Great Bible, to the popular Geneva Bible.[5] The Bible of 1611 arose accidentally from an effort at political compromise[6] after the union of the Crowns of England and Scotland, but its little note 'Appointed to be read in Churches' assured it a good start, and it did in fact hold the field for 300 years and more.

Now it has been surrounded with a host of other translations – J. B. Phillips, the New English Bible, the Jerusalem Bible, the Good News Bible – will they ever stop? Probably not. But in the meantime the Authorised Version had implanted itself firmly in the hearts and minds of the English people. As I write I find a great motor firm advertising its latest model as 'Something of a wolf in sheep's clothing', unknowingly quoting Matthew 7:15!

The first and obvious cause of this was the development of morning and evening prayer as the basic religious diet of the Church of England. It might have been otherwise; in most European countries it *was*. In England, however, those who went to church went on Sundays, mostly in the morning. After the discovery of gas-lighting they went in the evening. There they heard, year in, year out, the distinctive language and rhythms of early seventeenth-century English, 'a well of English undefiled'. No one can exaggerate the effect of this sociological phenomenon on the people. Two very different examples may be given. Readers of P. G. Wodehouse will remember how Bertie Wooster was always in danger of relapsing into biblical phrases. He certainly shows no sign of being a mature Christian or Bible student (hardly a member of BRF!) but he belonged to a circle of upper middle-class folk whose place was in church on Sunday mornings. The 'Great Sermon Handicap' is a lasting reminder of a period now long over.

An example of a very different kind comes from Lord Hailsham's autobiography *'The door wherein I went'* (Collins, 1975). Speaking of the influence of the Bible on his life he writes (p. 71):

'Looking back on my life I find that the Bible in its coherent entirety has been one of the main influences on my character and conduct. I believe this is true of everyone who has come into contact with it and has not deliberately chosen to disregard its message. My own contact with it became peculiarly intimate in the years between 1950 and 1964 when after my father's death I was living at my home in Sussex and having to read lessons Sunday by Sunday at Herstmonceux where we worshipped. It is impossible to read the Bible out loud week after week without finding the immense power and vitality of almost every part of it. It seems to come to life and movement on your lips like a living thing. It almost wriggles like a fish on the line, like a snake in the hand. It is not a dead word, but a living word. Of course I like best the magic language of the Authorised Version. But the experience is the same whatever version is used.'

To estimate, however roughly, the impact of the Bible on the English people during the last 300 years it is necessary to have some vivid *feeling* of what the regular reading in public of the Authorised Version has meant. Of course during the last 100 years or so private reading has come in to supplement the public reading, but it is the public reading which has gone into the veins of the English people.

Perhaps the matter can be summed up thus – the people came to live their lives against a back-cloth of a great drama, beginning with creation, going on through the story of the Hebrew people, continuing with the gospel story, carrying on with the great Pauline passages, and concluding with the pictures of heaven in the Revelation of St John the Divine. Of course, after the Industrial Revolution, church attendance slumped horribly. The nation lived more and more on its spiritual and cultural capital. But the heritage was there. Like an old mansion, somewhat overgrown and neglected, it remained as a mark of identity for the English people. The English people never quite ceased (until modern times) to be the people of a book, and that book the Bible.

Part of the appeal lay in the particular quality of the English in which the message was enshrined. The language was old, it was elevated, it was more and more familiar. As each

4

Sunday came round, certain sentences and paragraphs came up with unfailing regularity. If I may quote an example, trivial in itself, I remember vividly when I was about 15 years of age hearing a fine old priest of the old school coming to the end of the Genesis 42, the story of Jacob reluctantly consenting to allow Benjamin, his youngest son, to accompany his brothers to Egypt for corn, as Joseph had demanded. I can hear the ringing tones now, ending with a great *rallentando*: 'If mischief befall him by the way in the which ye go, then shall ye bring down my gray hairs with sorrow to the grave'. From the point of view of style, one could point to the high proportion of monosyllables in the text, but the real point defies analysis. We are talking about language that has a sacramental quality – the medium is the message.

Distinguished critics like Sir Arthur Quiller-Couch have gone into great detail about how the texture of the Authorised Version is made up. He once analysed Isaiah 60, verses 1–3: 'Arise, shine; for thy light is come, and the glory of the Lord is risen upon thee. For, behold, the darkness shall cover the earth, and gross darkness the people: but the Lord shall arise upon thee, and his glory shall be seen upon thee'.

Quiller-Couch ('Q' as he was known) started from the premise that 'I' sounds, short or long, imparted brightness or brilliance to the material, while 'O' sounds imparted grandeur and dignity. So the combination of the two produced a kind of diapason dignity, shot through with a kind of flute-like cheerfulness. How far this verbal harmony was born in the ear of the listener it is hard to say; all I will say is that I never hear this passage without thinking of Q's analysis.

It cannot be overlooked that the passage just referred to forms one of the great *arias* in Handel's *Messiah* and nowhere does the vowel-music of the passage come over more strongly than when sung by a great soloist. In fact the relation between the Authorised Version and the great oratorios is itself a matter of considerable interest. It might be said that the whole *schema* of the Bible, the story of Creation and Redemption has been injected into the blood of the English people *via* the music of Handel and Haydn. Not of course that only through this medium could its message be heard.

Who can exaggerate the influence of Luther's German version of the Scriptures on the German people? Who can overestimate the importance of the Latin version upon St Augustine, or of Ulfilas's[7] specially made Gothic version upon the wild tribes of south-east Europe in the fourth century? And yet . . . Who can judge what has been the effect of 'I know that my Redeemer liveth' as the words rang out at the beginning of every funeral in England for 300 years? Or who can say whether the actual words 'Suffer the little children to come unto me' have not vividly implanted a doctrine of baptism, right or wrong, in the minds of ordinary worshippers? As a bishop I can state categorically that people of every social and intellectual structure have shown themselves familiar with these words and deeply attached to them.

So it has to be faced that the English mind and English letters have been shot through with a rich and varied literature, ultimately dating from Old and New Testament times. Some of it is clothed in immortal prose – e.g., the closing verses of 1 Corinthians 15: 'So when this corruptible shall have put on incorruption, and this mortal shall have put on immortality, then shall be brought to pass the saying that is written, Death is swallowed up in victory . . .' Sometimes the biblical material has entwined itself with the ordinary language in a much more subtle way. Thus Keats, writing of the song of the nightingale, imagines that he hears the self-same song that found a path

> Through the sad heart of Ruth, when sick for home,
>   She stood in tears amid the alien corn.

Perhaps one statement could be made without much fear of contradiction. The long history of the Hebrew people, with its early sagas, its unique story of the escape from Egypt, its long-drawn-out battles to secure possession of 'the promised land', its moving poetry, its 'public oratory', followed by the totally different story of Jesus, his teaching and his death and resurrection, has proved able to incorporate itself into the literature and culture of many different lands and continents. Some may think that this reveals something of its universal appeal, and even of its supernatural quality, but we will make no sweeping assertions of this kind at the moment. All we will say is that, through translation, Hebrew and Hellenistic literature have implanted themselves inextricably in the literature of the world.

Notes

1. One edition of the Bible was even entitled 'The Bible, designed to be read as Literature'! (Ed. and arranged by E. S. Bates, London 1937.)

2. Aramaic was originally the language of Aram (Syria), but was used as the trading language throughout the Middle East. It was a language belonging to the same group of languages as Hebrew and Phoenician. The portions of the Old Testament written in Aramaic are Ezra 4:8 – 6:18; 7:12 – 26; Daniel 2:4b – 7:28.

3. The title *Apocrypha* literally means 'hidden' and is really a misnomer. The collection includes mainly historical and wisdom writings as well as additions to the books of Esther and Daniel.

4. This translation is called 'Authorised' because it received authorisation from King James I, the project having been put forward at the Hampton Court Conference in 1604. It is often called the King James Version, although he was not a contributor! It was really a revision of earlier translations.

5. Two versions of John Wycliffe's (*c.* 1329–84) Bible exist, the first dating before 1382 and the later version belonging to the period between 1395 and 1408, issued after his death.

William Tyndale (*c.* 1494–1536) produced his translation in 1525 in Germany, as he had had to flee from England because of his Lutheran sympathies.

The Geneva Bible was produced about 1560 by British Protestants in exile in Switzerland (including John Knox). It is often called the Breeches Bible because of the translation of Genesis 3:7, where the word 'breeches' is used as the article of clothing made by Adam and Eve from fig leaves.

6. King James I unsuccessfully tried to bring Scottish Presbyterians and English Episcopalians together!

7. The ancient Goths founded an empire north of the lower Danube and the Black Sea. Christianity was brought to them by captive Christian priests seized during Gothic invasions of Asia Minor in the middle of the third century AD.

Ulfilas (born *c.* AD 311) was the son of a Cappadocian mother and a Gothic father. (His name means 'little wolf'.) Created bishop in AD 341 he worked among the Goths, created a Gothic alphabet and translated the Scriptures into his native tongue. The most famous copy is the Codex Argenteus, probably made for the king of the Ostrogoths in Northern Italy in the early sixth century. It is now in Sweden.

2: Deep Mines of History

This chapter has nothing to do with the well-known question, so dearly loved by amateur archaeologists, 'Is the Bible true?' It rather approaches the problem from the other end. Thousands of people read the Bible with the minimum equipment of historical, archaeological or linguistic knowledge. But in doing so they acquire considerable familiarity with whole tracts of history and geography otherwise unknown to them. Like John Bunyan, a man of minimal literary acquaintance, who from his regular reading of the Authorised Version became one of the great literary figures in English history, so they have obtained 'the freedom of the centuries and the continents' from their reading of the Bible.

Let us explore something of what this means. Forgetting about such arbitrary dates as 4004 BC[1] (the one-time traditional date for the creation of the world) a casual glance shows that the 'history' of the Old Testament covers the period from the time of the Pharaohs to the setting-up of the Hellenistic kingdoms after the reign of Alexander the Great. Although some glimpses are given of life in a wider environment, the story is laid for the most part in the south-east corner of the Mediterranean littoral. It is with the impact of the great powers of Egypt, Syria and Babylon on the little nations of Judah and Israel that the story is concerned. Apart from the patriarchal narratives and the records of the early occupation of Canaan, which both look to the second millennium BC, most of the history covers (approximately) the period from 1000 BC to 165 BC – quite a span!

What can we learn from all this? We must first put into a separate category the creation stories. The earliest 'centre of gravity' for the Israelites as they looked back over history was not the creation but the deliverance from Egypt (see Deuteronomy 26:5–9). The story of the deliverance, however, carried with it the miracle of the Red Sea being parted for the Israelites, and closing on the Egyptians. This indicated that the God of history was also the God of nature. Hence there arose stories which taught that their God (Yahweh) was also the God of creation. Canaanitish sources have shown that there were traditions native to that land with which some of the creation stories have verbal links. The great opening chapter of the Bible, written much later than the Genesis 2 story, may have been influenced by what they had learned during the 'long exile on Babylon's strand'. Verbal links with Babylonian stories also exist. Any attempt to square these stories with modern post-Darwinian sources is doomed to failure. In spite of that there is a majestic dignity in the story in Genesis 1, where formlessness yields to form, darkness to light, and emptiness to all the variety of vegetable, animal and human life. The writers knew nothing of evolution, but they understood the pageant in which every form of life had its appointed place.

As to the wanderings of the patriarchs, no one knows what basis of historical fact lies behind the hallowed traditions. All we know is that the Hebrew people firmly believed that their God had called Abram out of Ur, into the promised land, and that around the story of his wanderings the fundamental folk-lore of the people had been built.[2]

The Nile clearly dominates the life of Egypt. So much is clear once the Israelites have made their way from Canaan to that land. The conditions of slavery described in the early chapters of Exodus easily suggest how, at other times, the Egyptians were able to build the Pyramids and the Sphinx. Once the Jews had escaped from Egypt, a fact that clearly dominated the whole mentality of the Israelites for centuries (as can be seen from Psalms like 105 and 106) their subsequent history consisted of a long period of independence, then their trampling down as the armies of Assyria and Babylon swept over them, destroying their sanctuaries and dominating their peoples. An acquaintance with the books of Kings and Chronicles opens the windows of the mind to the ebb and flow of the great powers of the eighth and seventh centuries BC, of which poor little Israel (and later Judah) were the unwilling victims. The prophets attach moral values to the changing fates of Israel (Jeremiah is an obvious example) but at this distance in history it is legitimate to ask whether any moral changes, for good or bad, could have affected the onward march of the armies, each destined in turn to overcome its predecessor.

An interesting glimpse into the psychological repercussions of these political upheavals can be seen in Psalm 137 – 'By the waters of Babylon we sat down and wept'. Here we have some local colour to start with: we are reminded that Babylon is a city built by the river-side; that the waters are slow-flowing (so different from the tumultuous streams and *wadis* of Israel); that the Israelites were homesick ('How shall we sing the Lord's song in a strange land?'). If we needed corroboration of the story in 2 Kings 24 (and elsewhere) we should not have to look further. Incidentally, the Psalm shows the intensity of the trauma experienced when their land had been ravished and unspeakable atrocities committed against old and young alike. No wonder that there is the horrific explosion of hatred for the Edomites who joined in like jackals: 'Happy shall he be that rewardeth thee, as thou hast served us'.

The pictures of the liturgical ceremonies given in the Old Testament are particularly interesting. Naturally these show strong resemblances to the sacrificial cults of the surrounding peoples, but there are striking differences. The Jews had no 'idols'. In the Holy of Holies the wings of the cherubim hovered over the 'covenant box', the almost empty symbol of God's Presence with his people. Daily sacrifices culminated in the annual Day of Atonement, when with elaborate ceremony the High Priest entered into the Holy of Holies, there to make expiation for the sins of the whole people. In such ways did the Jews keep alive the idea that sin was a serious matter, and that its expiation was something of grave concern. Alongside the growing importance of the central sanctuary in Jerusalem came the prohibition of worship at the local shrines.[3] Any Bishop who has tried to close a modern (or ancient) church will well understand the reluctance with which the Jews contemplated the loss of their local 'high place'.

Many will have come across their first vivid picture of a primitive agrarian civilization from their reading of the Bible. If we leave out the nomadic, sheep-rearing economy of the pre-Canaanite days we are given endless pictures of life as it was lived – e.g., in Bethlehem round about 1000 BC. Here we see the ever-present threat of famine, causing Naomi and her family to emigrate to Moab, across the Jordan. Then the return, after the loss of all the men-folk in the family. The faithfulness of Ruth is expressed in immortal words, which have deservedly become part of the Jewish marriage service. Then comes the typical 'harvest home' celebrations, and the eventual acceptance of Ruth as a wife of Boaz. This is confirmed by a 'meeting of elders' sitting at Bethlehem's gate, a scene which is re-enacted to this day, as any traveller to the Middle East can testify. Ruth, the Moabitess, is incorporated into the family of which David is to be born.[4] Here, then, is all the material for the study of civilization in a very early period. It does not provide a highly academic sociological study, but it provides material for a 'direct-method' study of great value. The man who 'knows his Bible' well can move with confidence over large tracts of the ancient world.

The fate of Israel will itself give the reader some inkling of the struggle of the great powers for possession of the 'fertile crescent'. It is in fact instructive to see how even to this day the little land of Israel lies like a shuttlecock between Egypt on the one hand, and Syria on the other, with Iraq playing the part of Babylon in the background. But the immediate lesson is to see how Israel of old lost her sovereignty and, being banished to Babylon, developed as a *church* rather than as a *state*. It is not too much to say that the whole phenomenon of Israel as a religion, with all that this has meant in the modern world, arose from the loss of independent sovereignty by Israel.

With the rise of Persia, relative autonomy was restored to Israel, as was also the life of the successive Temples. From this arose not only the Temple cult, with its influence on the Christian theology of atonement, but also the gathering into one book of the various collections of Psalms, with all that they have meant in the emergence of Christian hymnody.

The efforts of the Hellenistic kings, especially Antiochus Epiphanes, to obliterate Judaism led to a successful revolt under Judas Maccabaeus and to almost a century of renewed independence.

Towards the end of the Old Testament period the Jews began to spread around the Mediterranean coast. This brought them into touch with the vaguely philosophical thought of the Egyptians, and this is reflected in the 'Wisdom'[5] literature, parts of Proverbs, Wisdom itself, and Ecclesiasticus. As much of this survives only in Greek, a case could be made out for treating it with the Greek part of the Bible, i.e. the New Testament, but as the thought of the New Testament is distinctive, and related to Jesus of Nazareth, it will be more convenient to treat it here.

It must be squarely faced that we shall not find in the Bible anything that fits in literally with a modern scientific view of the universe. Although some biblical writers were roughly contemporary with Aristotle, they lacked any scientific classified strata, showing how the universe was made. What *is* true is that they had their own stratification, and it was not a bad one. Look, for instance, at 'The Song of the Three Children', which is found in the Apocrypha, and also in the Book of Common Prayer, where it often replaces the *Te Deum* during Lent and Advent.

The 'Song' provides a very interesting survey of the plan of the universe as the writers and his contemporaries saw it. Of course, at the head of it all stands God himself – 'O all ye works of the Lord, bless ye the Lord.' If we now extract from each verse all but the important noun we get the following sequence: angels, heavens, waters above the heavens, powers of the Lord, sun and moon, stars of heaven, showers and dew, winds of God, fire and heat, winter and summer, dews and frosts, frost and cold, ice and snow, nights and days, light and darkness, lightning and clouds, the earth.

At this point the song turns from the great forces of the universe and works steadily through the more 'pedestrian' elements in the earth's make-up: mountains, green things (cf. the grassy alps below the snowy peaks), wells, the sea, living things in the sea, fowls of the air, cattle, men, Israel, priests, 'levites', spirits of the righteous, humble men, and finally three actual individuals. Ananias, Azarias, and Misael.

Behind this framework can be seen the way in which the Hebrews pictured the universe, a great system in which every part had its appointed role in making up the chorus of praise to God its Creator and sustainer.

The book of Job in its later chapters offers a striking picture of the world of nature as the author saw it. His theme is the greatness of God's creative power, compared with man's puny strength. Job was not present when God set limits to the sea, and said, 'Here shall thy proud waves be stayed'. Job cannot 'bind the sweet influences of Pleiades, or loose the bands of Orion'. The great animals, especially the sea-monsters, the *behemoth*[6] are quite beyond Job's conception or creative power. The whole passage (chapters 38–41) gives a very vivid picture of what the world of nature looked like to a seeing eye. Job has some similarities with a Greek tragedy, but whereas Sophocles is staggered with the inventiveness of man, Job is humbled at the thought of man's littleness as he confronts God face to face.

So here again 'the well is deep'. To immerse oneself in the pages of the Bible is to gain the freedom of one of the great literary traditions of the world – not so polished as the Greek or Roman, but nevertheless far in advance of the trivial trash with which the bulk of modern man is regaled on TV and in the Press.

In Proverbs and Wisdom one can pick up ideas of the scientific outlook of the times. Take, for instance, this passage from Wisdom 7:16ff.

> In his hand are both we and our words;
> All understanding and all acquaintance with divers crafts.
> For himself gave me an unerring knowledge of the things that are,
> To know the constitution of the world, and the operation of the elements;
> The beginning and end and middle of times,
> The alternations of the solstices and the changes of seasons,

The circuits of years and the positions of stars;
The natures of living creatures and the ragings of wild
  beasts,
The violences of winds and the thoughts of men,
The diversities of plants and the virtues of roots:
All things that are either secret or manifest I learned,
For she that is the artificer of all things taught me.

No doubt the actual information available under all these headings was very patchy, and probably included a good deal of legendary or superstitious material. But the actual headings would not have made a bad syllabus for the Natural History Tripos at Cambridge!

Or consider these words from Wisdom 11:24ff.

Thou lovest all things that are,
And abhorrest none of the things which thou didst
  make;
For never wouldest thou have formed anything if thou
  didst hate it.
And how would anything have endured, except thou
  hadst willed it?
Or that which was not called by thee, how would it
  have been preserved?
But thou sparest all things because they are thine,
O Sovereign Lord, thou lover of men's lives.

These words would have done for an ecologist's or a conservationist's charter! It is indeed remarkable that at about 200 BC, or a little later, there should have been so clear an understanding that all things depend on God for their survival. But the passage leaves many doctrinal or philosophical questions unanswered. Does God desire the maintenance of malarial germs or of malignant cells? These questions were out of range of the primitive scientists among the later Hebrew (or Greek) writers. All we need note is how deeply they had already penetrated into the structure of the universe, and into the mutual dependence of its many constituent elements.

How real and fascinating this biblical history has become to those who study it may be illustrated from a passage in William Hazlitt's famous essay, 'My First Acquaintance with Poets'.[7] The essayist is describing, in a rather condescending way, his father's endless study of fusty old volumes dealing with biblical history. The young Hazlitt, who was drawn to philosophy, finds his father's concentration on the ancient history of the Bible strange and unattractive, but the 'Dissenting Minister' in the lonely Shropshire countryside felt differently. 'He passed his days' says the son, 'repining but resigned, in the study of the Bible and the perusal of the commentaries – huge folios, not easily got through, one of which would outlast a winter! Here were "no figures nor fantasies" – neither poetry nor philosophy – nothing to dazzle, nothing to excite modern curiosity; but here to his lack-lustre eyes there appeared, within the pages of the ponderous, neglected tomes, the sacred name of JEHOVAH in Hebrew capitals . . . glimpses, glimmering notions of the patriarchal wanderings, with palm-trees hovering on the horizon, and processions of camels at the distance of 3,000 years; there was Moses with the Burning Bush, the number of the Twelve Tribes, types, shadows, glosses on the law and the prophets; there were discussions (dull enough) on the age of Methuselah . . . questions as the date of the creation, predictions of the end of all things . . .' Hazlitt finishes this long passage (here much abbreviated) thus: 'My father's life was comparatively a dream: but it was a dream of infinity and eternity, of death, the resurrection, and of judgment to come.' He was writing of the year 1798.

We must now turn to a totally different set of documents, those we describe as the New Testament. These emerge from a different period of history (shall we say AD 50 to 100?) and they are written in a kind of popularised Greek, that which spread over the eastern Mediterranean after the victory of Alexander the Great over Darius III in 333 BC. It is not necessary to go through all the dynastic quarrels between the descendants of Alexander, but merely to state that by 44 BC Palestine had come completely under Roman rule. The first four books of the New Testament (or certainly the first three) emerge from the same geographical area as the books of the Old Testament; the other books have a wider *provenance*. They represent letters (mostly real letters, but partly improvised ones) circulating among the cities of Asia Minor, and including one long letter purporting to be addressed to Rome itself. They all spring from the events and teaching of a travelling Rabbi, Jesus of Nazareth, whom his followers believed (and still believe) to have been crucified for their sins, and to have risen from the dead 'on the third day'.

My point now is that there is no way of learning history like the study of first-hand documents. Thousands of people read, and have read the New Testament who have had no opportunity to study Roman history, or conditions in ancient Palestine. But they have learned, and still can learn, a great deal about these things by the careful reading of documents with which they are already familiar.

Let us begin with Luke 3:1–2. Here Luke, who makes a real effort to set his story in a proper historical context, sets the historical background for his gospel.

> 'Now in the fifteenth year of the reign of Tiberius Caesar, Pontius Pilate being governor of Judea, and Herod being tetrarch of Galilee, and his brother Philip tetrarch of the region of Ituraea and Trachonitis, and Lysanias tetrarch of Abilene, in the high-priesthood of Annas and Caiaphas, the word of God came unto John the son of Zacharias in the wilderness.'

This is an instructive passage. It shows first of all that the gospel story is located in the great Roman Empire. Tiberius had not measured up to the stature of Augustus, but he had held together one of the greatest empires in human history. As to the immediate environment, the territories had been divided up – Pontius Pilate, for ever commemorated (albeit ingloriously) in the Creed, was governor of Judaea (and Samaria) and other princelings held surrounding tracts of country, such as Galilee and Trachonitis. Religion was in the hands of Annas and Caiaphas. Only one (Caiaphas) could be High Priest,[8] but Annas, his father-in-law, having held the office for many years, seems to have acted as a kind of deputy. This was the setting for the beginning of John the Baptist's mission in the wilderness.

The study of the gospels opens up all kinds of windows on Jewish life and religion during the first century.

It so happens that there is very little other evidence (apart from that in the New Testament) concerning the various parties and sects within Judaism in the first century. Josephus[9] certainly tells us quite a lot in his *Antiquities*, but his evidence does not notably differ from that in the gospels. So it is that we can learn from the gospels about the Sadducees, who accepted only the books of the Jewish Law, and not the Prophets and who therefore rejected the doctrine of life after death; of the Pharisees, descendants of those who fought against the Hellenising customs of Antiochus Epiphanes (165 BC) and of the Herodians, of whom apart from the fact that they clung to the Herods, we know little. The one group that has come into prominence during recent years are those who wrote and preserved the Dead Sea Scrolls. These may have been Essenes, of whom we read in Josephus, but not in the gospels. Some of the ideas, however, that are prominent in the Fourth Gospel, are also prominent in the Dead Sea Scrolls, and possibly John the Baptist himself had some affinity with the Essenes, or with the Dead Sea sect.

There was the continual tension between the teaching of Jesus and the rigid observance of the Jewish law. Prominent among points of tension were the food laws, the keeping of the sabbath, the attitude to the Temple cult. Broadly speaking the message of Jesus was 'I will have mercy and not sacrifice'. The trial scenes bring out many more facts of life in Jerusalem. The Sanhedrin (the High Priest's Council) was concerned with the charge of blasphemy, and with messianic claims. Pilate's court was concerned with the death penalty, and with any claims that might challenge Caesar's undoubted supremacy.

When one passes from the gospels to Acts, one travels widely between Jerusalem and Rome. Everywhere Roman officials are in evidence, noticeably in Cyprus, Philippi, and Rome itself. Sometimes local officials (like the Asiarchs at Ephesus) have a measure of authority. Where there is evidence of an archaeological kind (as in the case of the 'town clerk' *(grammateus)* at Ephesus Acts 19:35) the local colour is surprisingly accurate. The final chapters give us a vivid picture of sea-faring life and methods in the first century AD.

The letters move in a circle of important towns and cities,

and give the reader an eye-opener into a side of life which would otherwise almost certainly escape him.

In the Bible, then, we have two ancient cultures, one Hebrew (1000 BC to 165 BC), one Hellenistic (AD 50 to 100). One concentrates on Palestine, but spreads out to the great powers of 'the fertile crescent'. One concentrates on Judaea and Galilee, but does not end until it reaches Rome itself.

Notes

1. This was the dating of James Ussher (1581–1656), Archbishop of Armagh. His *Annales Veteris et Novi Testamenti* (1650–4) provided the dating which was inserted in the margins of the Authorised Version from 1701 onwards.

2. Recent archaeological excavations have illuminated the patriarchal period for us. The recent finds at Ebla in Syria (1974–5) show that the patriarchal names were fairly common personal names from 2300 BC onwards.

3. Whilst some shrines were more important than others (e.g. Bethel, Shiloh, Gilgal), once Jerusalem had been captured by David (2 Samuel 5:7) and the Temple built there (1 Kings 6) by Solomon, the shrine there gained in importance until *c*. 622 BC (under King Josiah) other shrines were compelled to close down.

4. It is possible that the story of Ruth was written up to counteract the more exclusive legislation of Ezra and Nehemiah in the fifth century BC, which ruled out intermarriage. The Book of Ruth points out that even their greatest king had foreign blood! (Ruth 4:17–22)

5. Some of the Wisdom Literature goes back to the period of the early monarchy, when international influences were very strong. We have Wisdom writings from Egypt and Babylonia dating from the second millennium BC. The writings as we have them in their completed form probably reflect Greek thought as well.

6. The emphasis on the sea-monsters (Hebrew: *behemoth*) as being under God's control owes something to other (non-biblical) accounts of creation, in which the control of the monster of the deep is a symbol of God's creative power. The deep speaks of chaos and God's creative act of order out of chaos.

7. These chapters are being written during the bi-centenary of Hazlitt's birth in April 1778. (R.R.W.)

8. Originally the office of High Priest was held for life, but under Greek and Roman rule the king or governor showed his authority by dismissing High Priests and appointing others in their place. It is likely that Annas was not simply a deputy for Caiaphas, but recognised by many Jews as the *real* High Priest.

9. Flavius Josephus (AD 37 – *c*. 98) was a Jewish man of letters who proved his military skill in a small siege resisting the Romans, and then his larger diplomatic prowess in a career on the Roman side. He wrote in Greek a 'History of the Jewish Wars' and 'Jewish Antiquities (a history of the Jews down to AD 66).

3: Deep Personal Piety

To concentrate on the literary or historical aspects of the Bible would be to remain in the shallows of Scripture and not to 'cast out into the deep'. We read the Bible, publicly and privately, because we believe that through it God speaks to us, and gives us language in which we can speak to him. Of all the books of the Old Testament, the book of Psalms stands out as pre-eminent in its wealth of material clearly suited to these needs. Perhaps for that reason the Psalms are still frequently bound up with the New Testament in neat little volumes. This seems to imply that even when one has come to regard the revelation in Christ as the supreme gateway to fellowship with God, the devout words of men (and possibly women – who knows?) remain an invaluable assistance to the Christian as he tries to grow in grace and in the knowledge of God.

What is it about the Psalms that has won for them so unique a place in the devotional material available to the Christian?

First there is the personal nature of the language used. Look for instance at some of the early psalms and their first verses (our version is normally the Prayer Book one): 'Hear *me* when *I* call, O God of *my* righteousness' (4:1), 'Ponder *my* words, O Lord: consider *my* meditation' (5:1), 'O Lord *my* God, in thee have *I* put *my* trust' (7:1), '*I* will give thanks unto thee, O Lord, with *my* whole heart' (9:1). So we could go on for large parts of the Psalter. Scholars have debated for many years whether the 'I' of the Psalmists is really a personal pronoun, or whether it actually stands for Israel, the people of God. It is clear that the Psalms were used as the material for corporate worship, in the Temple and later in the synagogues, and in these circumstances the thoughts of the Psalms may have been 'transferred' to the whole people. In the main, however, I feel that the language is so vivid, the experiences so intimate, that the Psalms really are personal poems of prayer and praise. This has made them easily adaptable as prayers for individual Christians. So when a congregation sings 'The Lord is my Shepherd: therefore can I lack nothing' many individual members will take these words on their lips as an expression of their own personal trust and confidence in God.

Secondly the Psalms stand out because of their concentration on God, their God-centredness. Perhaps nowhere else in the Bible is the mind directed so uniformly to God himself. Nowhere else is man's praise of God expressed so continuously and so directly. There is no need to multiply examples, for one can open the Psalter almost anywhere and find the same thing. I open mine at Psalm 18:1 – 'I will love thee, O Lord, my strength; the Lord is my stony (strong) rock, and my defence: my Saviour, my God, and my might, in whom I will trust, my buckler, the horn also of my salvation, and my refuge'. The writer piles one metaphor upon another, in order to enumerate all the many aspects of God's protective power. Or take the shortest of all the Psalms, 117 – 'O praise the Lord, all ye heathen: praise him, all ye nations. For his merciful kindness is ever more and more toward us: and the truth of the Lord endureth for ever. Praise the Lord'. These themes are repeated again and again, particularly in the last group of Psalms in the book. God is intensely real to the Psalmists, and as we read their words, written so long ago, he can become real to us.

Thirdly, and this is an extension of the last point, the Psalms stand out for the intensity of the devotion they express.

They show an intense love for God's law. By this they meant primarily the *Torah*[1], in the sense of the first five books of the Bible. Some writers may have included other parts of the Old Testament. Although this love is expressed briefly in the second part of Psalm 19 it reaches its climax in Psalm 119, 'the long psalm', made up of a section for each letter of the Hebrew alphabet[2], each verse in each section beginning with the same letter. In every verse there is a reference to the law, or to the testimonies, or to the judgements, to the word, or the commandments of God. The writer pledges his whole-hearted devotion to God's revelation of himself as he understood it. 'The law of thy mouth is dearer unto me than thousands of gold and silver.' Not many of us would care to claim such devotion either to the Old and New Testaments, or to the records of the Word made flesh.

There is an intense love of God's house, the Temple at Jerusalem. This comes out strongly in 'the Songs of Degrees', the pilgrim psalms sung on the way to Mount Sion in annual or other pilgrimages (see especially Psalms 121, 122, 125). Psalm 84 is another outstanding example: 'O how amiable are thy dwellings: thou Lord of hosts! My soul hath a desire and longing to enter into the courts of the Lord: my heart and my flesh rejoice in the living God'.

There is an intense trust in God, in spite of adversity. One of the well-known examples is in Psalm 73. Here the writer contemplates the prosperity of the wicked, and begins to wonder whether it is in vain that he has 'washed his hands in innocency'. But then he goes 'into the sanctuary of God' (v. 16). In that setting he realises the temporary nature of the sinners' prosperity. He realises that he has been 'foolish and ignorant' (v. 21). He sees, after all, that God has held him by his right hand, and concludes, 'Thou shalt guide me with thy counsel: and after that receive me with glory ... My flesh and my heart faileth: but God is the strength of my heart and my portion forever' (vv. 23, 25).

So we shall not be surprised to find that there is an intensity of personal penitence. Though not unique, Psalm 51 will always be regarded as the supreme expression of penitence on the pages of Scripture. There is something very remarkable about this psalm – the intensely inward and spiritual understanding of what penitence means. The writer begins with an earnest prayer that God will 'wash him from his wickedness, and cleanse him from his sin'. He regards himself as tainted with sin from his birth, and sees that God requires 'truth in the inward parts'. It is a clean *heart* and a right *spirit* for which he prays (v. 10). Only if God 'opens his lips' can he hope to 'show forth God's praise'. The sacrifice that God wants is 'a troubled spirit', and God will not despise a contrite heart.

The ending of the psalm, which contemplates outward offerings of 'young bullocks' on God's altar, has every appearance of being an addition by some who thought the psalm had gone too far in the direction of rejecting the cultus[3].

Having seen some of the elements which have gone to make the Psalter 'a treasury of devotion', we might go on to see how the whole of *time* was seen as the sphere of worship and prayer to Almighty God.

I remember, when I was a very young man, perhaps still a boy, coming across a little volume of Bishop Andrewes' Devotions[4]. For one of his evening prayers he quoted Psalm 141:2: 'Let my prayer be set forth in thy sight as the incense: and let the lifting up of my hands be an evening sacrifice'. When I was taking Evensong at St John's College, Durham, I used to like to quote those words as an invitation to worship. Andrewes, of course, was a masterly exponent of prayer as a means of sanctifying *time*. He collated all the references to the hours of prayer – the third, the sixth and the ninth, from the Gospels and Acts; he noted our Lord's prayers in the dim dawn, and those which occupied the whole night.

There is no doubt that the early Christians adopted the principle of regular prayer at fixed times of the day – the *Gloria in Excelsis* is a very ancient hymn for Matins, *Hail, Gladdening Light* a similarly ancient one for the lighting of the lamps – both possibly dating from the third, or even the second century AD. The whole monastic system was based on the same idea. The 'Work of God', the *Opus Dei,* was chiefly that of praise and prayer.

The Rule of St Benedict (AD 525) clarifies and codifies what was already taking shape both in the secular churches and in the incipient monastic orders. Benedict says:

'As the prophet says, "Seven times a day do I praise thee." This sacred number seven will be fulfilled by us if, at Lauds, at the first, third, sixth, ninth hours, at vesper time and at completorium (compline) we perform the duties of our service; for it is of these hours of the day that he said "seven times a day do I praise thee" (Psalm 119:164). For concerning the night hours, the same prophet says, "At midnight I arose to confess unto

24

thee" (Psalm 119:62). Therefore at these times let us give thanks to our Creator, concerning the judgements of his righteousness.'

There is much interest in studying 'the clock and the calendar' in the Psalms. Of course there were no clocks, only sundials, and, for most people, just the sun itself, running its daily course (or so it seemed) and separating morn from eve, day from night. The 'Calendar' was mostly the sequence of the seasons – spring, summer, autumn, winter – but the priests calculated more exactly in order to keep the festivals and the sacrifices in line with the lunar cycle. We can look at the impact of clock and calendar on the Psalms, and extend this treatment to other sequences in life, such as sickness and health, youth and age, birth and death.

Let us begin with morning. The first 'quote' I notice is characteristic: Psalm 5:3 – 'My voice shalt thou hear betimes, O Lord: early in the morning will I direct my prayer unto thee, and will look up.' What better words could we recite as we begin our morning devotion, Matins, or whatever form it takes? And let no one think that it is easy to keep up even this elementary devotional discipline. Of course the Psalmist had no radio programmes, no newspapers or post – as also he had no hot-water supply or electric light! But he had grasped a vital point. 59:16 is similar: 'As for me, I will sing of thy power, and will praise thy mercy betimes in the morning', but here there is an implied contrast with the wicked, who 'in the evening grin like a dog, and run about the city'. 63:1 is classical – 'O God, thou art my God: early will I seek thee'. 'Early' can be interpreted in different ways – early in life, early in the day, early in dealing with each new project.

92:1–2 is similar, but here the morning praise is linked with that of the evening – 'It is a good thing to give thanks unto the Lord: and to sing praises unto thy Name, O most Highest; to tell of thy loving-kindness early in the morning: and of thy truth in the night-season'. The custom of starting and ending the day with prayer, and Cranmer's decision to bracket all the earlier offices in Matins, and the later in Evensong, had plenty of precedent, particularly in the Psalms.

I have always liked the reference to morning and evening

in Psalm 119:147–8 – 'Early in the morning do I cry unto thee: for in thy word is my trust. Mine eyes prevent (i.e. anticipate) the night-watches: that I might be occupied in thy words'. Here the stress is on the *earliness* of the devotion – early in the morning, and *before* the night watches fall. The latest translation is helpful: 'Before the morning light I rise and I call: for in your word is my hope. Before the night watch my eyes wake: that I may meditate upon your words'. In this Psalm the stress is on the importance of meditating on God's word, and these words fit easily into the Anglican tradition of giving much space in Morning and Evening Prayer to the reading of Holy Scripture.

Some of these passages have linked the evening with the morning as a time for praise and prayer, but some which concern primarily the evening deserve a mention.

3:5 refers to going to bed – 'I laid me down and slept, and rose up again: for the Lord sustained me'. 4:9 has the same idea – the words are familiar from Compline: 'I will lay me down in peace and take my rest – for it is thou, Lord, (thou Lord) only, that makest me dwell in safety', the last words being also familiar to us from S. S. Wesley's Introit 'Lead me, Lord'[5]. Psalm 119 naturally has various references, e.g. verse 55 – 'I have thought upon thy Name, O Lord, in the night-season', and verse 62, 'At midnight I will rise to give thanks unto thee: because of thy righteous judgements'. The latter verse was taken as the scriptural warrant for the monastic custom of rising for Matins and Lauds at 2 a.m. I often thought of it when I lived at Durham and visited Hexham Abbey. The thought of the monks getting out of their relatively warm beds and marching down the famous staircase into that stone-cold abbey church sent a sympathetic shiver down my spine! And we can end this series of quotations with the short and beautiful Psalm 134. Again it comes easily to mind from Compline, with its picture of those who 'by night stand in the house of the Lord: even in the courts of the house of our God'. The Psalm tells us to 'lift up our hands in the sanctuary', but we have allowed the Pentecostalists and the football fans to monopolise this particular expression of praise and thanks!

Psalm 55 (v. 18) has an anticipation of the three special *hours* of prayer – 'In the evening, and morning, and at noonday will I pray, and that instantly: and he shall hear my voice'.

Insomnia gets full treatment in Psalm 77 – 'Thou holdest mine eyes waking: I am so feeble, that I cannot speak' (v. 4). 'I have considered the days of old: and the years that are past. I call to remembrance my song: and in the night I commune with mine own heart, and search out my spirit' (vv. 5–6).

Then comes the famous dialogue, 'Will the Lord absent himself for ever . . . Is his mercy clean gone for ever . . . Hath God forgotten to be gracious?' And the triumphant conclusion, 'I said, It is mine own infirmity: but I will remember the years of the right hand of the most Highest. I will remember the works of the Lord: and call to mind thy wonders of old time.' A wonderful example of escape from self-centred depression into reliance on the unchanging power of God.

All this is to go on every day – as we see in Psalm 145:2, 'Every day will I give thanks unto thee: and praise thy Name for ever and ever'.

Several instances occur of the intention to carry on with praise to the very end of life, e.g., 63:5 – 'As long as I live will I magnify thee on this manner: and lift up my hands in thy Name'; 86:12 – 'I will thank thee, O Lord my God, with all my heart: and will praise thy Name for evermore'; 146:1 – 'While I live will I praise the Lord: yea, as long as I have any being, I will sing praises unto my God'. Words like these inspired Isaac Watts' great hymn[6] –

> I'll praise my Maker while I've breath,
> And when my eyes shall close in death,
>   Praise shall employ my nobler powers.
> My days of praise shall ne'er be past
> While life and thought and being last,
>   Or immortality endures.

John Wesley is said to have recited these words very shortly before his death.

The same idea is apparent in John Newton's 'How sweet the name'. After the thought that when he sees Christ as he is he will praise him as he ought, he goes on:

> Till then I would thy love proclaim
>   With every fleeting breath;
> And may the music of thy name
>   Refresh my soul in death.

The cycle of the seasons is not so clearly represented as that of each passing day, but it is there.

Psalm 104, the great nature psalm, shows it clearly. Verse 30 says, 'When thou lettest thy breath go forth they shall be made: and thou shalt renew the face of the earth'. Earlier verses make it clear what this implies. Springs are sent into the rivers; the beasts quench their thirst; the birds find shelter, and sing among the branches; grass for the cattle precedes the gifts of wine, oil and bread.

Fuller pictures of the harvest occur in the well-known sixty-fifth Psalm, as also in Psalm 144. This has a lovely picture of garners full of all manner of store, productive flocks of sheep, 'oxen strong to labour', and, best of all (and still elusive), 'no complaining in our streets'.

Infancy, youth and age all are represented. Psalm 71 is strong on the thought of God's care and providence from birth onwards; e.g., v. 5, 'Thou art he that took me out of my mother's womb'. (A slight variant comes in Psalm 22:9 – first the reference as in Psalm 71, then the words 'thou wast my hope, when I hanged yet upon my mother's breasts'.) 71:15–16 is striking – 'Thou, O God, hast taught me from my youth up until now: therefore will I tell of thy wondrous works. Forsake me not, O God, in mine old age, when I am gray-headed: until I have showed thy strength unto this generation, and thy power to all them that are yet for to come'. (A prayer that comes with special relevance to those of us who are approaching the end of their official ministry!)

Psalm 37:25 – 'I have been young, and now I am old' – was the subject of a great sermon in Great St Mary's, Cambridge, when Dean Vaughan went back there to give what was almost certainly his last University sermon – it is worth reading if you can pick up a copy. Psalm 90, verses 10 and 12, will get less familiar if Psalm 90 is altogether replaced at funerals by Psalm 23 sung to Crimond! It is important.

'The days of our age are threescore years and ten; and though men be so strong, that they come to fourscore years: yet is their strength then but labour and sorrow; so soon passeth it away, and we are gone . . . So teach us to number our days: that we may apply our hearts unto wisdom'.

Finally a few references to sickness and health. It is not always easy to discover exactly how to take some of these references. Many are so vividly expressed that they must, it seems, be taken literally. But some of them occur in contexts where the plight of the psalmist (or the righteous – usually, I must admit, the same thing!) is described in terms of being surrounded by enemies. Whether literally, or metaphorically intended, their interest for us is the same.

Psalm 22:14–15 is a case in point – 'I am poured out like water, and all my bones are out of joint: my heart also in the midst of my body is even like melting wax. My strength is dried up like a potsherd, and my tongue cleaveth to my gums: and thou shalt bring me into the dust of death'. All this is in the context of the man surrounded by enemies – human and bestial – and could not fail to be associated with the Passion story in the gospels.

38:1–10 gives another concentration of physical woes – 'There is no health in my flesh, because of thy displeasure: neither is there any rest in my bones, by reason of my sin . . . My wounds stink, and are corrupt: through my foolishness . . . my loins are filled with a sore disease: and there is no whole part in my body . . . My heart panteth, my strength hath failed me: and the light (sight) of mine eyes is gone from me'. It is clear in this case that the writer looks on his troubles as the result of sin – a common Old Testament view, as instanced by the friends of Job. But thoughts of bodily weakness are intertwined with language about enemies laying snares, and it is difficult to decide where description ends and metaphor takes over.

Fortunately recovery is represented, as well as illness, though not so regularly and vividly. We have 103:3, 'he healeth all thy diseases', and a rather fuller picture in 107:18–21, 'Their soul abhorred all manner of meat: and they were even hard at death's door. So when they cried unto the Lord in their trouble: he delivered them out of their distress. He sent his word, and healed them: and they were saved from their destruction. O that men would therefore praise the Lord for his goodness: and declare the wonders that he doeth for the children of men!'

Such quotations may whet our appetite to look out for the many other gems of devotion, often disguised by much useless material in which they are set. The quotations cover a huge field of literature, and a vast period of time. Taken together they give a vivid picture of a certain type of piety. It was a piety mixed up with much self-pity, much self-righteousness, much criticism of enemies, and prayer for God's vengeance to be poured out on them. There is much for Christians to avoid, as well as to emulate. But when all is said and done, we have here a wonderful example of a way of life in which God's immediate presence, at all times and in all places, was recognised and realised. Morning, noon, and night, all day, every day, in sickness and in health, in prosperity and adversity, in the fellowship of God's people at the Temple, in the silence of midnight in the bed-chamber, he was there, ready to hear both the praises and the prayers of those who called upon him.

Our revelation of God is richer. Our response is usually much poorer. Calvary and Easter are more than the equivalent of the Exodus and the Red Sea. But here is the call coming down through the ages – 'I will alway give thanks unto the Lord; his praise shall continually be in my mouth'. This note of continual prayer and praise is frequent in the New Testament – 'Men ought *always* to pray and not to faint', 'Giving thanks *always* for *all* things' – but how many of us come anywhere near this ideal?

So we have to pray, with the seventeenth-century hymn-writer, John Mason:

> 'I shall, I fear, be dark and cold,
>   With all my fire and light;
> Yet when thou dost accept their gold,
>   Lord, treasure up my mite.'[7]

Of one thing we can be certain, and that is that when our Lord read and used the Psalms he could do so with complete devotion to the will of God, in a way that we can never aspire to do. There are a number of allusions or vague references to Psalm language in the words of Jesus as recorded in the gospels, but the two principal examples both come from the Cross itself. St Mark records the bitter cry of desolation from Psalm 22:1 – 'My God, my God, why hast thou forsaken me?' – and this apparently unanswered question brings Christ very near to all those who through pain or anguish of spirit feel impelled to use the same or similar language. St Luke records the last words of Jesus as a quotation from Psalm 31:5 (6 in Prayer Book version), 'Into thy hands I commend my spirit'. But Jesus prefaces the words with the word 'Father' – doubtless 'Abba' when spoken. Thus our Lord takes the *personal* piety of the Psalms and transforms it into *filial* piety. Psalm 103 had likened God to a father who pities his own children, so there was a precedent there for the idea. But it is through the Son that we come to the Father, and it is the Holy Spirit, the spirit of adoption and sonship, 'whereby *we* cry, Abba, Father' (Romans 8:15).

Notes

1. The word *'torah'* cannot easily be translated into English. It indicates God's *direction* for life or divine *guidance* in a specific problem, but then comes to mean the codified form of divine legislation for man's need and so the first five books of the Bible (Pentateuch), because in them is contained the understanding of God's direction for Israel.

2. Hebrew poetry generally was fond of using puns and acrostics. Monsignor Ronald Knox, in his translation of the Psalms, has tried to preserve the alphabet basis of Psalm 119 and calls it 'An Alphabet of Loyalty to the divine Law'. Compare Psalms 111 and 112 for a similar play on letters.

3. The *cultus* refers to the sacrificial and ritual side of Israel's religion. It is likely that all the psalms presuppose the regular background of Israelite worship and ritual.

4. Lancelot Andrewes (1555–1626) was successively bishop of Chichester, Ely and Winchester. His devotions or private prayers (*Preces Privatae*) were written in Greek and Latin for his own use and only published after his death – in 1648.

5. The first half of the Introit, 'Lead me, Lord, in thy righteousness' comes from Psalm 5:8.

6. For a sympathetic treatment of the hymns of Isaac Watts (1674–1748), see the next BRF Book Club volume—*Singing to the Lord* by Dr Michael Ball.

7. From *How shall I sing that Majesty*; in *English Hymnal,* No. 404.

4: Deep Memories of the Lord

It is obvious that the early Christians (by which I mean those who were living as adults, say from AD 30 to 60) lived deeply under the influence of the Lord Jesus Christ. But exactly how that influence made its impact upon them is a complicated question. We are apt to assume that they knew 'the gospels' as we know them. But did they? 'The epistles' (Romans to Jude) were written, say, from AD 50 to 100[1] (the latter date is highly arbitrary) and over this same period the four gospels were in process of formation. Yet there is hardly a direct reference in the letters to the exact statements of the gospels, and certainly none to their coming into existence as books.

It is a salutary exercise to consider how much (or how little) we should know about Jesus if we had no gospels, and were dependent on the letters for our biographical facts. We should know that he was 'born of a woman, born under the law' (Galatians 4:4), that he was of the seed of David (Romans 1:3), that he was characterised by 'grace', i.e. generous self-giving (2 Corinthians 8:9) and by 'meekness and gentleness' (2 Corinthians 10:1). That on the eve of his passion he 'started' something that became 'the Lord's Supper' (1 Corinthians 11:23–26, 20). From Hebrews 5:7 we learn of his supplications 'with strong crying and tears', a phrase that reminds of the gospel stories of Gethsemane. We should know that he died on a cross (Philippians 2:5–8, and repeatedly elsewhere). We learn, almost everywhere, that he rose from the dead on the third day (see especially 1 Corinthians 15:1–23 – and as the phrase 'he was raised' here follows the words 'he was buried' there is a strong presumption that a bodily resurrection is implied). We learn in Ephesians 4:9 that he 'ascended'. There is a brief reference to a saying of the Lord (that about divorce) in 1 Corinthians 7:10 and one to an otherwise unrecorded saying, 'It is more blessed to give than to receive' (Acts 20:35). And that is about all!

It can be said that the great assertions are the credal and doctrinal verities, rather than detailed reminiscences, stories, or teachings. You could compose the Apostles' Creed more easily from the epistles than from the gospels. Yet, during the years when the epistles were being written the gospels must have been taking shape. Like the epistles, they are written in Greek, so they must have belonged to the section of the Church which had emerged from its Palestinian chrysalis and was moving freely in the Hellenistic world of Christianity's 'first expansion'[2]. But their link with Palestinian origins is indisputable. The scene of their story is laid in Judaea, Samaria and Galilee. The local colour fits this environment. By AD 140, the time of Justin Martyr, 'the memoirs of the Apostles called gospels' were read at Sunday eucharists, and there is no reason to think that Justin was an innovator in this respect. By AD 170 the 'Canon'[3] of the New Testament, with gospels and epistles both included, was fairly definitely established. One can only guess that as the years increased between the earthly life of Jesus and the contemporary experience of the Christians, the movement to preserve in more detail the story of Jesus led to the editing and composing of the gospels.

It may be convenient here to summarise the 'conventional wisdom' about the dating of the gospels. Each date is the subject of unending discussion. Bishop John Robinson has recently advanced the view that most of the books were written much earlier than contemporary scholarship usually assumes[4]. But here we will accept the more usual views. Mark is usually placed about AD 65. 'Q' (if it existed!) was a document mostly consisting of sayings of Jesus, and was incorporated, in whole or in part, by Matthew and Luke, who also used a great deal of Mark. 'Q' may have been quite primitive. Both Matthew and Luke defy exact dating, but AD 80–86 are commonly thought of as possible dates, with Matthew slightly earlier than Luke. The Fourth Gospel stands in a different category. Though in the form of a gospel it assumes throughout the 'divinity' of Jesus, and the doctrine of salvation to eternal life through faith in him. It may well be much later than the other gospels, and AD 90–100 is a common dating. Recent scholarship tends to attach more historical value[5] to its material than was commonly the case, and the discovery of a papyrus extract dating from AD 140 has finished the wild ideas that were once common of a date well into the second century.

So, by the beginning of the second century, the Church had, in addition to the vivid letters of Paul and others showing the main outlines of primitive Christian faith, much fuller documents filling in the details of the life, work, death, and resurrection of the Lord. Doubtless, still, the Church's principal link was with the Living Lord, exalted to heaven, still bearing 'those dear tokens of his passion', present through his Spirit in the congregations and in the hearts of believers. But alongside this 'mystical union' was a mass of material that made possible 'an extension of the Incarnation', in the sense that the Christian could, as it were, follow Jesus through Galilee and Samaria, hear his words, see his deeds, watch him die, and be made aware of his mighty resurrection. This was to affect deeply the subsequent nature of Christian experience and Christian life. They now had 'a framework' into which to fit their knowledge of his earthly life. Whether Mark's gospel really gives such a framework is still debated. Some hold that the gospels consist of a number of 'bits', incidents and sayings as used by teachers and preachers, and that their arrangement in Mark is arbitrary. Against this is the obvious fact that all four gospels end with the death and resurrection, so it is not surprising that two begin with the birth, one (John) with the eternal status of 'the only-begotten Son of God', and one (Mark) with the mission of John the Baptist. I hold that there *is* a framework.

In addition to the framework we have a large number of miracle-stories, great blocks of teaching, increasing disputes with the religious leaders (the Scribes and Pharisees) and very long detailed accounts of the final trials and of the Passion and Crucifixion. Vivid pictures of the Resurrection appearances conclude each gospel, with the possible exception of St Mark, where the text is doubtful.

Such, it may be held, is a very brief and rough summary of what most scholars believe to be the facts relating to the four gospels, and to their relation to the epistles. To those who are thoroughly familiar with the epistles they remain in the sub-conscious mind of the individual Christian, when he reads, or hears read, the gospels. But how far do these 'scholarly' facts affect the reader in his face-to-face confrontation with the gospel material? Judging from my personal experience, only to a very limited extent. I do not parade this as a virtue, but I have tried to be honest in my appraisal. That they have *some* effect, I shall freely admit, and shall try to clarify what that effect is. But I believe the direct impact of the gospels to be a personal matter, and perhaps no two readers are affected in quite the same way.

To be factual I fear that here I must be to some extent autobiographical. My own background, in childhood and early youth, was what is now summarily described as 'con-servative evangelical'. It is difficult to exaggerate the extent to which in such circles concentration was afforded to St John's Gospel, as we then usually called it. This was because the gospel was a direct challenge to personal faith, and it asserted without question the exclusive claim of Christ as the agent of salvation. John 3:16 ('God so loved the world . . .') was treated (and not unfairly) as the supreme summary of the gospel. God gave, through love, his only Son, so that all who believed in him should have eternal life. Many texts giving similar direct statements were clustered around this one. A notable one was John 1:12 – 'As many as received him, to them gave he power (authority) to become the sons of God'. 'Receiving him' was made equal to 'believing on his name'. The story of Nicodemus, with its stress on the new birth, was central. To my immature mind John 6:37 ('Him that cometh to me I will in no wise cast out') was a favourite reference, because I argued that however inadequate my 'belief in' or my 'receiving of' Christ I was quite sure that I had at least 'come' – approached in hope and trust the One who was the Saviour of the world. Looking back on all this, I feel that the Christ of whom I was told so much was presented just as 'the means of salvation' – this bore little relation to what he was and taught, although there was a link between his death and his power to save. I do not regret my youthful religious experience, for without it I might have had no other, but I have to face its limitations.

The truth is of course that the fourth gospel assumes the broad facts known and presented by the other three gospels. Read St John in the light of the others, and the challenging summaries about life and death, perishing and having eternal life, accepting and rejecting, fall into place. Great allegories pervade the book. The life of Christ is the best wine, the water of life which he gives springs up eternally, the feeding of the five thousand becomes the symbol of the life, the flesh and blood, which he gives for the life of the world. The blind man gets his sight, and this means that all Christians must rely on 'the light of the world'. He dies as the Passover Lamb ('not a bone broken'). His saving work is finished. The direct challenges remain; the firm promises remain. But 'the Son' is not just an 'idea'. He is Jesus of Nazareth, seen in his true identity. St John will always be a great evangelistic tool for the Church. This is why it was written. 'These are written, that ye may believe that Jesus is the Christ, the Son of God; and that believing ye may have life in his name' (John 20:31). Modern scholarship adds point to the challenge. It does not detract from it.

If I persevere on a personal note, the next milestone in my personal encounter with the gospels came when I began reading Theology at Cambridge just about 50 years ago. This milestone was a totally new interest in the first three gospels, especially St Mark. It is true that even then, in the teaching of Sir Edwyn Hoskyns (afterwards embodied in *The Riddle of the New Testament* by Hoskyns and Noel Davey)[6] there was a growing sense that St Mark did not present a figure of merely human dimensions, but one who was recognised, at least by spirits, as 'the Holy One of God'. The Christ of Mark was seen to be a dynamic figure, through whom God was mightily at work. But this could not disguise the great contrast between Mark's Christ and John's. Here was a figure unmistakably human; here there were definite phases in his story – enormous response from 'the common people', bitter hostility from the religious authorities. Here was a book that could be subjected to processes of literary and historical criticism, and it was. The personality of Jesus, even if it could not be minutely analysed, took on a definite form and colour. I bought a picture of Christ, walking with his disciples through the cornfields – a picture which I still have over my dining table – to symbolise the advent of this vivid historical 'Being' into my life. Mark 10:32 became a kind of key-word for St Mark – 'They were in the way, going up to Jerusalem; and Jesus was going before them: and they were amazed; and they that followed were afraid'. This vivid picture summed up the almost pre-destined journey to Jerusalem, the determination of Jesus to press on to the end, and the mixture of loyalty and bewilderment that characterised the disciples.

When it comes to Mark's Passion narrative, it is stark and unrelieved. Only one cry comes from the Cross: 'My God, my God, why hast thou forsaken me?'

Gradually one came to grips with the other two synoptic gospels – Matthew and Luke. At first one concentrated on the literary problems raised by the three documents that had so much in common but so much in each case that was distinctive. Then came the period when 'form criticism' ruled the day. Here one looked for short items of narrative or short pithy sayings of Jesus that could be easily memorised and used in teaching and preaching. 'Extreme' form critics valued this approach so much that they rejected the idea of a continuous narrative altogether, believing instead that the various items had just been strung together like beads on a necklace. Now there is a return to what is called 'redaction criticism', that is, attention to the editorial habits and style of each evangelist. Since the days of earlier synoptic study the tools of criticism had been sharpened, and scholars began to identify individual words and phrases as characteristic of each writer. It became easier to guess which pieces had come originally from the mind and pen of the writer concerned, and which were more likely to have been 'borrowed' and incorporated.

When, however, it comes to personal experience and to the devotional use of a book like St Luke, these scholarly niceties begin to play a much smaller part.

By way of illustration I mention some of my own reactions to the gospel of St Luke. I have always found this book to be particularly attractive. It has been called 'the most beautiful book in the world', and such I have found it to be. Let me give a few examples.

It begins with 'the infancy narratives' (as indeed so does St Matthew). But Luke's story grips the imagination even of a careless reader. The message of the angel to the shepherds in the fields outside Bethlehem is unforgettable. Sober historical judgement raises all kinds of questions about 'what actually happened'. The whole thing, in theory, might be a poetic expansion of Hebrews 1:6 – 'When he bringeth his firstborn into the world he saith, "And let all the angels of God worship him" '. But the poetry lifts the whole thing out of the realm of cool calculating historical examination. It was part of the writer's picture of what happened at the birth of the Saviour. It has entered deeply into the minds and hearts of nineteen centuries of Christian people. The Christian firmly believes that there was born that day a Saviour, who is Christ the Lord. The setting has become inescapably real. Whether the reality is similar to that of the thunderstorm in King Lear, or that of the battle of Waterloo, is in the last resort of minor importance. To me it *is* real, and always will be.

Luke has a human sensitivity which pervades his whole story. Christ's love for the sinful, the outcast and despised is embodied in a number of vivid and moving incidents, and in some the humanity of Christ himself is closely involved.

The story of Christ's visit to the Nazareth synagogue in chapter 4 is characteristic of Luke's picture of Jesus. As he faces his relatives, friends and neighbours, he takes his stand on Isaiah 61:1–2 – 'The spirit of the Lord is upon me, because he has anointed me ('Christed me') to preach good news to the poor . . . to proclaim release to the captives . . . and recovering of sight to the blind'. All such gracious works are recorded in the gospel, and veracity is confirmed by the plain and challenging words which follow these words of grace. So we come, in Luke 7 (after many of the Marcan miracles have been described) to the story (peculiar to Luke) of the restoration to life of the dead son of the widow of Nain, a little Galilean township lying just off the Nazareth to Tiberias road. Stress is laid on the human elements in the woman's suffering – the dead man was an only son of his mother, and she was a widow. Into this situation Jesus steps. He touched the 'bier' – perhaps the litter on which the body was carried, or perhaps a wicker coffin. Christ often touched what was considered untouchable (cf. Luke 5:13, the leper). Historically, the raisings to life are the hardest for our modern, scientifically conditioned minds to accept. There are no tests by which we can get nearer to the events than the accounts we have in the gospels. All I can say is that the love and compassion of our Lord's action here described has long been one of the incidents to draw from me such gratitude and love for our Lord as I have experienced.

And how impoverished would our gospel-picture be without the skilfully-grouped parables of Luke 15! We speak of the lost sheep, the lost coin, and the lost son. Perhaps we should speak of the seeking shepherd, the seeking housewife, and the seeking father. Anyway, the welcome afforded to the prodigal son will always remain the supreme parable of the loving Father of all, always 'on the look out' for his erring children, and always ready to surround them with welcoming and joyful love. To such open-hearted forgiveness they are in turn called, and the surly elder son in the story remains a standing example of how *not* to react in such circumstances.

In the same gospel (ch. 7 again) we have the story of the penitent woman, who could not restrain the display of her grateful love for Jesus. The Lord explains that it is all because she had been forgiven much and therefore 'loved much'.

When we come to the Passion narrative the story contains many touches of human compassion, and of an almost child-like trust in God. Here it is that Jesus prays as he is crucified, 'Father, forgive them'. Here it is that there is a word of hope for the repentant thief. Here it is that Jesus dies with the evening prayer on his lips – 'Father, into thy hands I commend my spirit'. Here it is that we have the wonderful story of the walk to Emmaus in chapter 24, with its many foreshadowings of Christ opening up the Scriptures, and being known in the breaking of bread, both of which should happen in every eucharist.

These are only isolated examples of the human love and

graciousness of the Lucan Christ. It is considered fashionable to 'play down' St Luke, on the ground that he softens the original 'scandals' of the gospel story, and has no understanding of the deep significance of the Cross as a redeeming sacrifice. I believe this view to be superficial but the matter cannot be argued out here. All I will say is that I know my own attachment to Jesus as Lord to have been stirred in me very largely through St Luke's picture of the One who did all things well, and like whom no other man ever spoke.

Notes

1. Much of our dating of the New Testament writings is conjectural. Bishop Williams provides the dating given by much New Testament scholarship. Recent writing, however, has tended towards an earlier dating than was once conventional; see the author's comments on pp. 34–35.

2. At one time there was a tendency to contrast the epistles as *theological* with the gospels as *historical* documents. Now we would see all the New Testament writers as having a deep *theological* concern.

Whilst you can speak of the Church as originally Palestinian or Aramaic-speaking, Greek culture was strong in Palestine, too. Recent writers are inclined toward the view that Jesus and his disciples knew Greek, even though Aramaic and Hebrew were their more customary languages, just as a Welshman would know English as well as Welsh.

3. The *Canon* (or definitive collection of New Testament books) was only fixed towards the end of the fourth century (possibly at the Council of Carthage in AD 397) – but the books included were commonly accepted as authentic for centuries before.

4. The reference is to the book *Redating the New Testament* by Bishop John Robinson (SCM Press, 1976). He would date all the books of the New Testament before AD 70. His chief argument is the silence in the New Testament about the Fall of Jerusalem (in AD 70). He argues that the fifties were the really great period of early Christian writing.

5. Local Palestinian traditions were detected by C. H. Dodd in his *Historical Tradition in the Fourth Gospel* (Cambridge UP, 1963).

6. *The Riddle of the New Testament* (Faber & Faber, 1931) stressed the theological intention of the gospel-writers, indicating the importance of their assessment of Jesus as the Christ. More recent redaction criticism (which examines the way a gospel-writer *uses* his material) confirms the judgement of Hoskyns and Davey.

5: Deep Reflections on the Faith

'O the depth of the riches both of the wisdom and the knowledge of God! how unsearchable are his judgements, and his ways past tracing out . . . for of him, and through him, and unto him, are all things. To him be the glory for ever.' Such are the words of St Paul (in Romans 11:33–36). No Christian has ever plumbed those depths as fully as he did in his letters, and through the continual reading and study of those letters in the Church, over some nineteen hundred years, his explorations have been shared with those of every century, and more recently, of every continent.

The letters of the New Testament, still often called 'the epistles' are very different from most of the letters that most of us encounter. In the ancient world there was no 'printing or publishing' in our sense of the words. Everything had to be written out by hand on papyrus or vellum. Creative thinkers tended to pack their 'theses' or reflections into documents that were cast in the form of letters to particular persons or groups. Some of them were, of course, real letters, occasioned by the need to communicate news or views from the writer to some destination. One such letter, that of Paul to Philemon is not much longer than the sort of letter one gets nowadays. It deals with a particular situation – how Philemon is to treat his returning, now Christian, runaway slave Onesimus, but it deals with this human situation in such a delicately Christian way that it has been thought worthy to have a place in the New Testament 'canon'. The letters to the Galatians and to the Corinthians deal similarly with concrete questions concerning Paul's apostolic relationship with them, but in their course they throw immense light on the life of the early Church and contain much teaching that has been of permanent value to the Church[1].

When we come to Romans, we are in rather a difficult atmosphere. There is still the letter form, especially at the beginning, but there is a little doubt as to whether the true text limits the readers to the Christians in Rome, or whether it may originally have had a wider audience. But in any case the letter has much more the appearance of an elaborate treatise than of anything that we should normally associate with a letter. It runs to 16 chapters, and scholars debate as to whether it originally stopped at the end of chapter 16, 15 or 14. Chapters 1–8 contain a powerful presentation of 'the gospel', of man's universal sinfulness, of Christ's perfect sacrifice and satisfaction, of the nature of life in Christ, and of the liberating power of 'the Spirit'. Chapters 9–11 are a kind of parenthesis on the past, present and future of the Jewish people, while from 12 onwards some of the ethical consequences of Christian faith are delineated. It has proved one of the most influential books ever written, and was, among other things, a principal influence on Martin Luther at the time of the Reformation.

Ephesians takes us into yet another realm. Here there are serious doubts as to whether the letter was originally addressed to the Ephesian Christians, or whether it was a circular letter. Personal notes are missing. The letter is closely related to Colossians, and most scholars think that Colossians is the earlier of the two. Possibly it came from 'the Pauline school' rather than from the hand of Paul himself.

However that may be, here we have a 'mountain-top' view of the Christian religion. The writer sees the universal Church as a whole, and sees it in the perspective of eternity, the object of God's foreseeing Providence since the foundation of the world, and the vehicle of his glory in the eternity to come.

These are just a few of the very varied documents that are all bound together in our New Testament as 'the epistles of Paul the Apostle'. Even Hebrews, which few scholars think Pauline, has the same ancient title, and Hebrews has only a faint flavour of a real letter, and that mainly in its closing verses. There are, of course, several other letters, bearing the names of Peter, James, John and Jude.

Up to about 50 years ago, it was common for scholars to write books on what they called 'The Theology of the New

Testament'. I myself benefitted from just such a book (by the American, G. B. Stevens[2]) when I was an undergraduate. Some more recent scholars, such as Alan Richardson and Stauffer, have also tried to present a unified theology by following through different theological themes in the New Testament. But they were running against the tide, for, whilst using the title 'Theology of the New Testament', writers since Bultmann[3] have tended to stress the *separate* and *multiple* theologies within the New Testament – those of the four evangelists and the various figures in the apostolic world – and especially the *changing* theologies to be found within the writings of one writer – St Paul being the only one to give us enough material to exhibit various phases in one man's experience and development.

In spite of all this there is a great deal of common ground in the various writings of St Paul, and much of this is shared – whether expressed in similar or dissimilar language – with other writers in the New Testament[4]. To put things briefly and crudely, they agree in their conviction that Jesus was *man*, and they use language about his relation to God that makes it reasonable to say that in their view he was 'divine', i.e. standing in such close relationship to God the Father as to be 'bracketed' with him, whether as Son to Father, or as his 'express image', to mention only two typical figures that are used. They agree that he died, in some sense 'for sin', and that he rose from the dead. They accept the fact of his Ascension and his heavenly reign. They look for some kind of future triumph and manifestation of his glory. These are major agreements, and in my view completely outweigh the undoubted differences of approach between the writers.

Let us begin with a brief exploration of the 'reflections' of St Paul on these deep matters.

(a) **The Cross.** To a Jew it was a major problem that the Saviour to be proclaimed had died by crucifixion, a form of death that carried a curse from the Old Testament, and great ignominy in the Hellenistic-Roman world. The Christians *had* to find a way of presenting this that would in some way 'neutralise' this scandal without abolishing it. So we find, at the beginning of Galatians (1:3–4) that 'our Lord Jesus Christ gave himself for our sins, that he might deliver us out of this present evil world, according to the will of our God and Father'. So here was a *purpose* for the death defined ('for our sins'), a consequence (deliverance from this present evil world) and a context – the will of God the Father.

How did St Paul, or his instructors, reach these insights? We do not know. But we can make some intelligent guesses. Paul was an educated Old Testament scholar. Among the chapters on which he meditated surely Isaiah 53 must have been prominent. To be honest there are only five allusions to this chapter in the whole of St Paul's writings, and some of these are not particularly exact. But it is in this chapter that we have the picture of a servant of God, who appeared to be forsaken by God, but whose sufferings were for our transgressions, his stripes 'the chastisement of our peace'. I feel quite sure that the early Christians found here the principal key to the enigma, why did Jesus die as he did?[5]

But Paul certainly drew on other parts of Scripture for further light. In Romans 3:21–26 he draws on the imagery of the Day of Atonement, and sees Jesus as set forth by God to be a *hilasterion*, an expiation, an atonement, or a place of atonement (a 'mercy seat') by means of which we may be justified freely by putting our faith in Jesus.

In 2 Corinthians 5:18 to 6:2 it is the concept of reconciliation that holds the field. God was 'in Christ reconciling the world to himself', and the Christian preachers are ambassadors, urging men to accept the offer. Paul uses very strong language just here. He says that God made Christ 'who knew no sin', to 'be sin on our behalf, so that we might become the righteousness of God in him'. This is what the Reformers called 'the marvellous exchange' implied by the gospel. It does not mean that Christ was made 'sinful', but that he was so enveloped in a sinful situation that he was in some sense identified with it, so that we might be enveloped in his goodness and obedience.

(b) **Creation.** The meditations of St Paul took him further back still.

The question was bound to arise as to who this Jesus really was. Everybody knew that he was a man of Galilee, but how could 'an ordinary man' have been the means of 'such great salvation'? His relationship to God was close and filial. The word 'Abba' (a homely word for 'Father') was constantly on his lips. Sooner or later someone had to speculate on whether he had an eternal relationship to God, whether, as later ages would have said, he was 'within the Godhead'.

St Paul did it, in Philippians 2 and Colossians 1, not to mention hints in earlier works. In Philippians 2:5–11, he makes the bold assertion that Christ 'was in the form of God', but willingly accepted all the consequences of humanity, and of suffering humanity at that. He became obedient unto death, even a death on a cross. In Colossians 1:13–17 we find still bolder thoughts. Once more all is linked with 'our redemption, the forgiveness of our sins'. But he goes on to say that this redeeming Christ is 'the image of the invisible God, the firstborn of all creation; for in him were all things created, in the heavens and upon the earth, things visible and things invisible . . . all things have been created through him, and unto him; and he is before all things, and in him all things consist (i.e. hold together)'.

Some of these ideas come from the Wisdom literature, particularly from Proverbs and Wisdom. Here was a picture of 'a master-workman' standing by God as his agent in creation. The Christians had been brought so close to God by Christ's redemption that they could imagine none other as his eternal 'wisdom' than Christ their Saviour.

(c) **Consummation.** St Paul's reflections were not limited to the eternities of the past: they extended to the eternities of the future. In Ephesians (we will count it as Pauline for our purposes) chapter 1, after a very clear reference to the Christians being chosen 'before the foundation of the world', he again starts from the 'redemption and forgiveness' (v. 7) that was the trigger for the great Christological passage in Colossians 1:14, but this time he goes forward as well as backward. He sees God's intention 'to sum up all things in Christ' (1:10). He sees the Holy Spirit (1:13) as the 'credit-note' for our inheritance. He prays that the readers may know what is 'the hope of his calling, what the riches of the glory of his inheritance in the saints'. He sees the exaltation of

Christ as the first stage of a process whereby all things are to be made subject unto him.

Romans 8:28–39 is moving in a similar realm of ideas. It would take a book to expound this one passage, but I may just say that in my view these verses contain the very quintessence of the gospel. God's gift of Christ is seen as the guarantee of a love and power that can make us all 'more than conquerors through him that loved us'. 'Nothing can separate us from the love of God in Christ Jesus our Lord' – a striking assertion of the uniqueness of Christ.

(d) **The Church.** St Paul gives us enough material to enable us to see fairly quickly how he thought of 'the church'.

He uses the word in two senses: (1) for local churches (2) for the one great Church. 'The church of God which is at Corinth' (1 Corinthians 1:2) is an example of the former use, 'Head over all things to the church' (Ephesians 1:22) an example of the latter. Church (Greek *ecclesia*[6]) means 'the called out', hence assembly or congregation. From the Corinthian epistles, one can learn much about the life and customs of the primitive Church. From the Pastoral Epistles (whatever be their relation to Paul) one can see an incipient 'church order', with bishops and deacons and widows, and with recommended procedure for the conduct of worship. He could not have contemplated a Christian outside the Church. *All* were baptised into one Body.

(e) **Consequences for daily life.** Many of the letters go beyond vague generalisations, and give detailed instructions on moral questions. 1 Corinthians 13 is an example of 'general principle' instruction. It is a chapter which has made the deepest impression on generations of Christian, and even non-Christian, people. Nowhere is there a more beautiful and delicate explanation of *agapē*, Christian love, with all its characteristic generosity and selflessness. In 1 Corinthians we have detailed instructions about divorce, shopping in a heathen market, and many other problems, some of which had been put to Paul in a letter from the Corinthian church. The later part of Ephesians gives us 'household tables', lists of people who owe a certain obligation to each other – parents to children, children to parents, husbands to wives, masters to servants, and so on. 'The Imitation of Christ' was a power-ful ethical constraint. 'Even Christ pleased not himself' – so we must not expect to please ourselves either. We are bought with a price.

All this may seem to indicate a fairly fully developed Christian community, and in some ways it does. But we must remember that the Pauline letters, many certainly genuine, some possibly written by members of 'the Pauline school', are among the oldest Christian documents that exist. The impact of Paul's conversion on a powerful mind, well-stocked with rabbinic knowledge, produced that sense of 'the depths of the wisdom of God' which we noted at the begin-ning of this chapter.

Although in the Authorised Version 'Hebrews' still bears the title 'The Epistle of Paul the Apostle', hardly anybody now thinks that it came from his pen. Origen's remark 'As to who wrote it, God alone knows' sums up the findings of scholars of many generations. But that it contains deep reflections on Christian faith is undeniable.

It starts with one of the fullest and most far-reaching descriptions of the Person of Christ to be found in the Bible.

Christ is described (in the opening verses) as 'a Son', 'the heir of all things, by whom also he made the world', the exact image of God, the outshining of his glory, the one who 'upholds all things by the word of his power' (compare Col-ossians 1:17), the one who personally 'purged our sins' and has now taken his place at God's right hand. Passages like this compelled the Church, by the fourth century, to express unambiguously its faith in Christ as one with God.

Most of the 'letter' consists of a detailed comparison bet-ween the sacrifices and the priesthood of the Old Testament system, and the 'one sacrifice for sins for ever' offered by Christ in his life, his suffering and death, and the eternally effective Priesthood of Christ, who has entered once for all into the Holy of Holies, the presence of God, to make inter-cession for us in 'the power of his endless life', enriched as it is by his perfect obedience, sealed with the shedding of 'his own blood'. No subsequent thought about the death of Christ and its meaning for all men can ignore the eloquent and moving chapters on this subject in Hebrews. Not for nothing has the Church continually turned to these chapters for special reading in Holy Week and on Good Friday.

This book also has deep insights into the nature of Christian faith. Here it is not so much the laying hold of an offer of 'justification' by God's grace as a faculty of interior vision, the power to endure 'as seeing him who is invisible', as Christ had done. Faith here gives substance to things only hoped for, and evidence beyond that which is available to the outward eye (Hebrews 11:1) The eleventh chapter gives a great roll-call of Old Testament heroes who have lived by this principle. Abraham, for instance, 'looked for a city which hath foundations, whose builder and maker is God'. Some of these thoughts have almost a Platonic ring about them, and the wonderful passage in the *Republic* (Book 9: In heaven there is laid up a pattern of 'the city' which he who desires may behold, and beholding may take up his abode there) contains many parallels in Hebrews. Here was a writer who called on Greek thought (no doubt mediated to him after earlier use by people like Philo) and conscripted it into the service of the gospel. St Thomas Aquinas was later to do the same thing with Aristotle, when *his* thought, through Arab influence, was becoming current coin in western Europe in the thirteenth century.

In the epistles then it is very plain that 'the well is deep'. We have not examined the three letters of 'John' with their re-inforcement of the 'black and white' presentation of the gospel in the book commonly attributed to St John – 'He that hath the Son hath the life; he that hath not the Son of God hath not the life' (1 John 5:12). We have neglected the two letters ascribed to Peter, and of course 'James' and 'Jude'. The lasting value of some of this material may vary. It is harder for modern man to make his own some of the wilder speculations of, say, Jude, than it is with the more timeless letters of John. But there is always *something* worth grappling with. To draw the water up from this deep well, we need patience, prayer, some concentration of thought. Modern translation may help, but it is not the language that is the real barrier. What we need most is the eye of faith, that shares the underlying conviction that 'to live is Christ'. The gospels tell us much about what Jesus was like. The epistles tell us what he means.

Notes

1. See *Something Overheard* by A. E. Harvey (BRF, 1977) for corroborating detail. He indicates that the New Testament provides us with material through which we can listen in on what was happening in the early Church.

2. G. B. Stevens, *The Theology of the New Testament* (T. & T. Clark, Edinburgh 1899; 2nd edition 1906).

3. R. Bultmann's *Theology of the New Testament* (SCM Press, 1952, 1955) does not try to unify the theology. He allows little to Jesus himself, but reckons that we have three normative forms of theology, that of the early Church, the theology of Paul and the theology of John. Alan Richardson, in *An Introduction to the Theology of the New Testament* (SCM Press, 1958) followed a thematic approach, as Stevens had done. In Germany, we have also had New Testament Theologies from E. Stauffer (SCM Press, 1955), Hans Conzelmann (*An Outline of the Theology of the New Testament*, SCM Press, 1969) and W. G. Kümmel (*The Theology of the New Testament*, SCM Press, 1974). Conzelmann and Kümmel, like Bultmann, do not see it possible to present a *single* theology – but stress a plurality of theologies within the New Testament.

4. A. M. Hunter, in his book, *The Unity of the New Testament* (SCM Press, 1943) stressed the basic themes in the *Credo* of the early Church.

5. C. H. Dodd, in his book *According to the Scriptures* (Nisbet, 1952) suggests that it was Jesus himself who drew the connection between the Suffering Servant in Isaiah 53 and himself.

6. In the Greek translation of the Old Testament this same word is used to translate the Hebrew word *qahal* which indicates Israel *assembled before the Lord*, having been called into being as a nation by him. The word *synagogue* (in the Greek) expresses a congregation, where the emphasis can be on the human initiative. By contrast the word *ecclesia* (like *qahal*) points to God's initiative.

6: Deep Longings for Life Eternal

'If a man die, shall he live again?' This question from Job 14:14 certainly expected, in its context, the answer 'No'. But it can be torn from its context and used to epitomise an almost universal longing, viz. for some assurance that physical death is not the final end. The longing may arise from different elements in the human experience. It may be just an expression of the love of life. 'Life is sweet, brother' says George Borrow, and however disappointing, even tragic and catastrophic, life may have become, most people cling to it, sometimes desperately. One answer to the inevitability of death is the assertion that beyond death is some form of continuing life – and at this point we need not distinguish between continuing life as some kind of immortality, and the bestowal of new life by some kind of resurrection. At a rather deeper level the hope of a life beyond this may reflect a true instinct, viz. the sense that the real person (the 'I' if we think of the first person singular) is something other than the sum of the parts of the visible body. Many races and many religions have had some conception of a state in which the 'real persons' of the dead continued to live in spite of the death and decay of the physical organism which was the vehicle or expression of the true self during earthly life.

As Christians frequently confess their faith in 'the life everlasting' we may profitably see how this faith is foreshadowed in the Old Testament and confirmed in the New.

An instructive story is that of King Saul's encounter with 'the witch of En-dor' in 1 Samuel 28. Saul's army was encamped at Gilboa (where he was to die in battle next day). The Philistines were in great strength nearby. Saul, in desperation, sought guidance from God, but none came. He had endeavoured to cut off 'wizards and witches' from the land, but in that last terrible night he decided to consult one. Going to En-dor he asked the 'wise woman' there to 'call up

Samuel', the prophet of his happier days. The woman sees 'a god' coming up from the earth, and the description assures Saul that it is Samuel. He puts his trouble to Samuel, but receives 'nought for his comfort', only assurance of defeat and death. Incidentally the story takes on a pathetic turn at this point. His *confidante* was not only a witch, but also a woman and now the woman in her overcomes the witch. She persuades the falling king to eat and rest. But it is difficult to read the story without feeling that the writer, and Saul, and his 'witch' (if the story has historical foundation) believed that Samuel was 'somewhere', somewhere in the abode of the dead, call it Sheol[1] or what you will, or he could not have been 'called up'. This view, of course, is similar to that of many adherents of primal religion, as in animist circles in Africa today.[2]

The Old Testament is mainly negative about the after-life. Some of the statements in the Psalms are definitely so. Consider, for instance, Psalm 88, 10–12: 'Dost thou shew wonders among the dead: or shall the dead rise up again, and praise thee? Shall thy loving-kindness be shewed in the grave: or thy faithfulness in destruction? Shall thy wondrous works be known in the dark: and thy righteousness in the land where all things are forgotten?' These questions certainly anticipate the answer 'no', particularly in the light of the context in the rest of the Psalm. Or again, in Psalm 115:17 – 'The dead praise not thee, O Lord: neither all they that go down into silence.'

Job 14:1–14 is an extended passage elaborating on the same theme. It begins with words very familiar to older English people, for they were always said at the graveside: 'Man that is born of a woman hath but a short time to live and is full of misery. He cometh up, and is cut down, like a flower; he fleeth as it were a shadow, and never continueth in one stay'. In Christian usage this applies only to mortal life, but in the Old Testament it was final. The writer goes on (in verse 7) 'For there is hope of a tree, if it be cut down, that it will sprout again, and that the tender branch thereof will not cease. Though the root thereof wax old in the earth, and the stock thereof die in the ground; yet through the scent of

54

water it will bud, and put forth boughs like a plant. But man dieth, and wasteth away: Yea, man giveth up the ghost . . . man lieth down and riseth not: Till the heavens be no more, they shall not awake'. This is pretty definite!

We must however look at some ambiguous phrases, and consider their import and history. The most famous is also in the book of Job, at chapter 19, verses 25 to 27. Again we know them from the funeral service. In another connection we have noted how many hearts have been warmed and strengthened when at the very entry of the funeral procession into church a voice rings out: 'I know that my Redeemer liveth, and that he shall stand at the latter day upon the earth. And though after my skin worms destroy this body, yet in my flesh shall I see God: whom I shall see for myself, and mine eyes shall behold, and not another.' In these words Christians have heard a summary of their ultimate faith in Christ, as the Risen Redeemer, destined to come in power, and to lead his own triumphantly into the presence of his Father. We may have to face the fact that in their first use they meant nothing of the sort.

Read the same passage in *The Good News Bible*: 'I know there is someone in heaven who will come at last to my defence. Even after my skin is eaten by disease, while still in this body I will see God. I will see him with my own eyes, and he will not be a stranger'. *The Good News Bible* has several footnotes saying 'Hebrew unclear', and it *does* give an alternative translation for 'while still in this body', viz. 'although not in this body'. In general, however, it translates on the basis that Job is talking of an experience he believed to be coming to him in *this* life. *The New English Bible* translates quite differently, building on the theme of the *Vindicator*, and contemplating divine intervention on his part in a court of law. *The Jerusalem Bible* begins by translating the crucial word (*goel*[3]) as Avenger, and does contemplate God's intervention after Job's death, and the belief that in some sense he will see this. The *Jerusalem* comment says that Job contemplates 'a brief return from Sheol' (the abode of the dead), thus preparing the way for a fuller belief in the resurrection of the dead. In the Vulgate, Jerome used the Latin word 'redemptor', which opened the way for a more 'Christianised' version in the English translations. In spite of all this, it is refreshing to go back to the eighteenth-century commentator, Matthew Henry. He had no doubt that the reference *was* to an experience after death, and aptly quotes Hebrews: 'They who said such things, declared plainly that they sought a better country, that is a heavenly' (11:14, 16). Could he have been right? In any case, though we must always try to discover the original meaning, there is no reason why words with one meaning should not become the vehicle of a richer faith in the course of years and centuries. There are many such cases in the Psalms.[4]

Or consider Psalm 16:10–12 – 'My flesh also shall rest in hope. For why? thou shalt not leave my soul in hell[1]: neither shalt thou suffer thy Holy One to see corruption. Thou shalt shew me the path of life; in thy presence is the fulness of joy: and at thy right hand there is pleasure for evermore'. As they stand, these words can carry a full-blooded faith in 'the life of the world to come'. But read them in the latest (Collins) translation of the Psalms: 'My flesh also shall rest secure. For you will not give me over to the power of death: nor suffer your faithful one to see the Pit. You will show me the path of life: in your presence is the fulness of joy and *from* (italics mine) your right hand flow delights for evermore'. It must be admitted that most modern translators are reluctant to see any faith in a life to come in most of the Old Testament writers and they *may* be biased, and hence led into all these 'this-worldly' renderings. But Christian faith, and Christian usage have certainly coloured the words, and the interpretation of the older versions. I notice that in the Soncino (Jewish) version and commentary it is stated that although the words have commonly been regarded as an 'intimation of immortality', the original meaning was different – deliverance *from* death, rather than victory over it.

Perhaps an important phase in the approach to a doctrine of resurrection was the development of imagery to express the hope that the nation of Israel would be resurrected and restored. The most well-known example is found in Ezekiel 37, 'the valley of the dry bones'. It is significant that this passage, though most clearly connected with a *national* resurrection, is read in the church lectionary during the Easter season. This might be justified on the ground that the old Israel sealed its doom by the rejection and crucifixion of Jesus, and that in the Resurrection of Jesus the New Israel was born, but the compilers of the lectionary probably were not so subtle. It is probable that the imagery of resurrection occurs so vividly that it becomes an *expression* of the possibility of the resurrection of Christians, anticipated as that is by the Resurrection of Christ.

The vision is familiar enough. The prophet envisages this great valley, filled with *very* dry bones. 'Can these bones live?' says God. Ezekiel says, 'O Lord God, thou knowest'. He is told to prophesy to the bones. He 'promises' the bones that God will put breath in them and clothe them with flesh. This happens in two stages – first the anatomical side is dealt with: bone comes to bone, and sinews and flesh are provided. Another prophecy brings life and breath. The resulting 'great army' is clearly stated to be 'the whole house of Israel' (verse 11). But note the language used to express God's interpretation of the vision – 'I will open your graves, and cause you to come up out of your graves, O my people; and I will bring you into the land of Israel. And ye shall know that I am the Lord, when I have opened your graves, and caused you to come up out of your graves'. Undoubtedly all this is part of a vivid promise of restored and renewed life for Israel, then largely in captivity in Babylon. But such language either indicates *some* conception of personal resurrection, or was likely to encourage such conceptions in the future.

However that might be, clear expressions of the hope of resurrection begin to appear in the last stages of Old Testament history. Under the impetus of the persecution of the Jews by Antiochus Epiphanes (168–165 BC)[5] the faithful began to see hope only in a resurrection *after* their torture and death. So we find in Daniel 12:1–3 these words: 'There shall be a time of trouble, such as there never was . . . and at that time thy people shall be delivered, every one that shall be found written in the book. And many of them that sleep in the dust of the earth shall awake, some to everlasting life, and some to shame and everlasting contempt. And they that be wise shall shine as the brightness of the firmament; and they that turn many to righteousness as the stars for ever and ever'. (Incidentally this last sentence is a splendid example of the prose rhythms which have marked the older English versions.)

In 2 Maccabees 7 a number of brothers are subjected to terrible tortures. One of them 'at the last gasp' says, 'Thou, miscreant, dost release us out of this present life, but the King of the world shall raise up us, who have died for his laws, unto an eternal renewal of life' (7:9).

This marks the climax of resurrection hope in the Old Testament, but before we turn to the New we must notice one other development. Greek thinkers did not contemplate *resurrection of the body* but *survival of the soul*.

It was not surprising that writings that emerged in the Dispersion, where Jews met Greeks, show traces of this feeling. Thus *Wisdom* gives us the famous words at the beginning of chapter 3: 'The souls of the righteous are in the hand of God, and there shall no torment touch them.' Ecclesiastes 12:6–7 is very familiar, read, as it usually is, on the last Sunday of the Church's year – 'Or ever (i.e. 'before') the silver cord be loosed, or the golden bowl be broken, or the pitcher be broken at the fountain, or the wheel broken at the cistern (four figurative expressions for death). Then shall the dust return to the earth as it was: and the spirit shall return unto God who gave it'.

Both ideas, resurrection and 'immortality' are made use of in the New Testament to convey different aspects of the Christian hope.

We now step over into the world of the New Testament. By now the most influential group among the Jews were the Pharisees, who had firmly accepted belief in 'the resurrection of the dead'. There might still be differences as to whether *all* were to rise again to judgement (the usual view), or whether the righteous only would rise, but in the main they had inherited and would pass on the hope which emerged clearly in the Maccabaean period that whatever happened here, all would be put right 'at the last day'. Against them were ranged the

Sadducees, a priestly sect that accepted only the first five books of the Old Testament ('the Law') and as there was nothing, at least on the surface, in those books about an after-life, they rejected the idea altogether.

This is the background of the story in Mark 12:18–27 where the Sadducees ask Jesus the 'trick question' about the woman who had seven successive husbands. 'In the resurrection' whose wife should she be, for she had had seven husbands? Jesus disposes of that question by saying that in the life to come 'there is no marrying or giving in marriage' but that was not the real point at issue. The real point was, 'Is there a resurrection at all?' On that Jesus takes them back to the story of the Burning Bush (recorded in Exodus 3, one of their accepted books). There God is described as the God of Abraham, of Isaac and Jacob. God, Jesus says, is the God of the living not of the dead. On this point therefore Jesus sides with the Pharisees against the Sadducees. Christ's answer was profound. It indicates that the only source of life, here or hereafter, is God himself.

There are three actual accounts in the gospels of 'raisings of the dead' by Jesus himself – the stories of Jairus's daughter, of the son of the widow at Nain, and of Lazarus. Modern man, with his sceptical, scientific mind, cannot help asking himself, 'Are they true? Did they really happen?'

The first two stand in a different light from the last, that of Lazarus. If we deal with that first we have to note that the Fourth Evangelist uses stories to dramatise truth. He moulds the historical tradition to make it a medium of the gospel. It would not surprise or alarm me if he had composed the story (or adapted a tradition that had reached him) to epitomise the great saying 'I am the resurrection and the life'. Jesus *is* the source of new life, and the story of Lazarus *may* be an acted parable. This cannot be positively asserted, but it is possible.

The other two incidents are different. They are much shorter and simpler. They occur in the story very naturally. They are not used in the gospels for any didactic purpose. If our scientific scheme of things is so much 'a closed circuit' that we cannot even allow the possibility of their happening, we must assume that they are pious legends, or wild exaggerations of something that really did take place. For myself, I see no reason to hold so negative a view. Which of us is in a position to say what is possible in the presence of the Son of God? This does not mean that Jesus was, so to speak, 'switching on his divinity'. Rather it means that man, when living in perfect harmony with God, may fulfil God's original purpose for man, and 'have dominion' over all that mars God's purpose of love for his children.

In any case, these 'small miracles' fade into insignificance before 'the great miracle', the resurrection of Jesus Christ from the dead on the first Easter Day. All the gospels (with the possible exception of Mark, whose text is doubtful after 16:8) end with this great story. Different versions are given; different incidents recorded. But all agree on the main fact – Jesus rose again, victorious over sin and death. All feeble gropings and hopings in the past now had their fulfilment. Man's greatest sin had become the vehicle for God's greatest demonstration of his love and power. Jesus 'showed himself alive by many infallible proofs'.

It is impossible here to embark on a full study of the Resurrection in the epistles. Perhaps two great passages from St Paul will suffice.

One is 1 Corinthians 15:12–19. Some of Paul's readers doubted the future resurrection. To them he says, 'If there is no resurrection, Christ is not raised. If Christ is not raised, Christian preaching is vain; faith is vain. If in this life only we have faith in Christ, we are of all men most miserable'. The resurrection of Christ is the cornerstone which holds together the whole structure of the Christian gospel.

Or consider 2 Corinthians 5:1–4. In the previous chapter Paul has re-affirmed his faith that 'he that raised up the Lord Jesus shall raise up us also with Jesus' (4:14), but in chapter 5 his thoughts take him in another direction. Having touched on the theme that 'the things which are seen are temporal, and the things which are not seen are eternal', he begins to think of the 'dissolving' of his earthly tent, presumably by death. If this comes, he has 'a building from God, not made with hands, eternal, in the heavens'. In this passage, he shows that the Hellenistic picture of the safe dwelling-place for the soul, when the body perishes, contributed *something* to his picture of the life beyond. 'To me to live is Christ', he said, 'and to die is gain'; 'to depart and be with Christ . . . is very far better' (Philippians 1:21, 23). All did not depend on resurrection at the last day, but this remained his basic conception (see 1 Corinthians 15:51 – 'We shall not all sleep, but we shall all be changed').

It would not be unfair to say that the whole epistolary section of the New Testament expresses not so much a *longing* for eternal life, but the certainty of its possession, with Christ and in Christ.

It is when we come to the last book of the Bible (Revelation) that we detect a very strong sense of 'longing' for divine intervention on behalf of the Christians, and for the glories of the life beyond the grave to which they looked as their deliverance from present troubles, and their compensation for all the evils they were experiencing. Revelation, according to the received opinion, was written at about AD 95, that is in the last years of the Emperor Domitian (AD 81–96), as a response to the sharply increasing persecution of Christians under that emperor. Domitian attached importance to the 'Caesar-worship' which served as a test of loyalty to the Imperial throne. The Christians could not participate in this without compromising their loyalty to Christ as King of kings and Lords of lords. Hence many suffered martyrdom. Their position was similar to that of the Jews under Antiochus Epiphanes 230 years before. Like the faithful Jews of that time they fell back on apocalyptic literature and speech as their reply. Both groups, Jews in 168–165 BC and Christians in AD 95, believed that God was revealing his purpose to them in this medium. Code language was used, to conceal the meaning from all but the chosen elect. Bold and far-reaching imagery was used. The sun could be darkened, the stars fall from heaven, the elements could 'melt with fervent heat'. But beyond lay the peace and glory of life with God, all perils past, all sins forgiven, all tears dried, all hopes fulfilled. Bishop John Robinson has queried the traditional dating, which goes back to Eusebius (fourth century) and in part to Irenaeus (late second century), and wants to put the date shortly before AD 70. If this should turn out to be correct we should have to replace Domitian with Nero as the arch-villain, but not many have yet fallen for this drastic 're-dating'. It would not affect the Christian value of the book.

The message of apocalyptic (and of 'The Apocalypse') is that help is coming soon. 'Behold, I come quickly', says the Lord (22:12). 'Even so, come, Lord Jesus', replies the writer. There is the hope, and there is the assurance of its fulfilment.

We must now look at the picture of heaven which is presented to us in Revelation. A clever sceptic once said, 'I can stand the Christian's hell, but I cannot accept the Christian's heaven'. Such remarks come naturally from those devoid of poetry and imagination, of whom there are all too many in our scientific world. Scorn is often poured on the prominence thought to be given to the playing of harps in Revelation's picture. Actually there are only four separate references to 'harps' in this long book, though one of these is a 'multiple' reference – 'harpers harping with their harps' (14:2). When it is remembered that in ancient times playing on harps was a natural expression of joy, one sees the point at once. (Compare the opposite experience of the Jews in exile – 'As for our harps, we hanged them up on the trees (willows) that are therein', Psalm 137.) But there are further adjustments to be made. Harps were a favourite Victorian instrument and as such come under the widespread scorn of all things Victorian. The Betjemanic Victorian revival has not penetrated to our twentieth-century 'mockers'. Again, there may be a different reaction when the 'anti-harp' league learn that the Greek word for 'harp' is *kithara*, and that this can be translated as *'guitar'*, to which it is etymologically related. If the translators had said, 'strumming on their guitars', they would have been equally accurate, and might have had a better reception in modern times!

All this is an unimportant digression. What we must face is that a great deal in the book *is* mysterious. Though scholarship can help us to discern the history of its imagery and phraseology (as it does) no one can say that the meaning and present relevance of all the chapters is clear to the casual, or even the careful reader. But shining through the tangled imagery there appear flashes of supreme insight, which have sustained in countless generations 'the hope of everlasting life'.

There is chapter 5, with its picture of the Throne of God. Here is the heart of all things, the Creator and Ruler of the universe. A lamb, 'as it had been slain' is 'in the midst of the throne' – an impossible combination maybe, but a vivid way of saying that the Cross of love reveals the heart and mind of the Ruler of all things. And there are 'seven lamps burning before the throne', 'the seven spirits of God', a poetical way of saying that the light of God and of the Lamb are always streaming forth to lighten the eyes and guide the minds of the faithful. Or there is the famous picture in chapter seven of 'the great multitude that no man could number' standing before the throne in their white robes, made white by the blood of the Lamb. Here was the inspiration of the wonderful picture by the Van Eyck brothers (in the Cathedral at Ghent) which some people have thought to be the most wonderful picture ever painted. The chapter also inspired, at a humbler level, Walsham How's popular hymn, 'For all the saints'. Christian life would be poorer without such art and poetry.

The book comes to its climax in chapters 21 and 22. Here is the picture of 'a new heaven and a new earth', 'the holy city, new Jerusalem, coming down out of heaven from God'. God will dwell with men (the final fulfilment of the hope registered at the birth of Jesus – Emmanuel, God with us). 'He shall wipe away every tear from their eyes; and death shall be no more.'

The further description of 'the holy city' is well worth study, but it is too long a task to attempt here. All the beautiful things known in that age – precious stones, gold and crystal – are used to portray the glory of God's eternal Kingdom. 'The Lamb is the light thereof' – our living Saviour – so Isaac Watts calls us to join, here and now, in that heavenly worship:

Come, let us join our cheerful songs
  With angels round the throne.
Ten thousand thousand are their tongues,
  But all their joys are one.

Worthy the Lamb that died, they cry,
  To be exalted thus.
Worthy the Lamb, our lips reply,
  For he was slain for us.

'His servants shall serve him, and they shall see his face' (22:3–4). In this world action and devotion have to be, at best, alternating phases of our response to God. Different religious orders concentrate on 'works of mercy' and on 'contemplation'. But there both are blended in one eternal, timeless response to 'him that loved us, and washed us in his own blood'. Alongside the confident lines of the eighteenth-century non-conformist may be placed the hopes of sad and wistful Peter Abelard (1079–1142):

Truly Jerusalem name we that shore,
'Vision of peace', that brings joy evermore!
Wish and fulfilment can severed be ne'er,
Nor the thing prayed for come short of the prayer.

Notes

1. The word *sheol* can also denote the 'grave'. At times it is translated by the word 'hell' but it is really the equivalent of the Greek *Hades*, expressing a sort of abode for departed spirits. There is no notion of punishment in the term, although it tends to point to a shadowy existence much slighter than ordinary life on earth.

2. The *animist* sees the Divine in the whole of nature. Many Africans will think in terms of constant communion between the living and the departed. See J. V. Taylor's *The Primal Vision* (SCM Press, 1962).

3. Originally the word *goel* stood for the kinsman who avenged the murder of his relative, but then was used of anyone who championed those who could not stand up for their own rights. God was, therefore, seen as the *goel* of the poor and the oppressed. In Job, to speak of God as Job's *goel* is to point to God's deep concern and Job's confidence that he has a kinsman in God himself. Job asserts that he is not deserted: he has God to speak for him no matter what happens!

4. Compare B. F. Westcott on *Hebrews* (Macmillan, 3rd ed., pp. vi-vii): 'No one would limit the teaching of a poet's words to that which was definitely present to his mind. Still less can we suppose that he who is inspired to give a message of God to all ages sees himself the completeness of the truth which all life serves to illuminate'. (R.R.W.)

5. The Book of Daniel reflects the time of severe persecution under Antiochus. The words of Shadrach, Meshach and Abednego point to the fact that the faithful may even face death for their faith (Daniel 3:17-18). God's justice, however, would demand the subsequent resurrection of those who had died for their faith. Hebrews 11:33-34 points to these stories of persecution and deliverance in Daniel, whilst Hebrews 11:35-37 gives further details of the severe atrocities perpetrated by the Syrian king Antiochus, mentioned in the Apocrypha.

Some readers may find part of the novel by James Michener, *The Source* (1965: Random House and Secker & Warburg) helpful in visualising the trauma of this period of persecution.

7: Drawing From The Well

The purpose of this book is to encourage readers to read the Bible for themselves with profit, and to profit from hearing the Bible read aloud.

There was an old teacher who gave this motto to Bible-readers: 'Apply yourself wholly to the text: apply the text wholly to yourself'[1]. That is the spirit in which to read and hear the Bible. Printed words will remain dead unless they are breathed into life by thought on the part of the reader, or by interpretation on the part of the preacher. It is when we have stopped reading and begun thinking that the Bible begins to do us good.

It is a help to see our passage in its context – both the broad perspective in which it stands, and the immediate setting in which it is placed. This book, with its broad sweep of interest, touching on literature, history, the story of Jesus and the faith of the early Christians may help us to know what kind of things to look for in any particular part of the Bible. We may find interesting literary or historical matter but most of all we want to be brought nearer to Christ. This may come as we study man's long hope for help ('Come, thou long-expected Jesus'), his experience and memory of the Incarnate Lord, and the deep teaching of the epistles.

If we are reading Mark we shall expect vividness; if St John, a clear statement of what faith in Christ involves; if Romans, the gospel of forgiveness through the Cross; if Revelation, the hope of Heaven. This is the closer setting of what we are reading. It will help us to look for the right things.

The worshipping life of the Church is another source of help. Down the ages the Church has associated certain parts of the Bible with certain seasons, and thus with certain doctrines of the faith. Read carefully Hebrews 1, and ask yourself why it is read as the Epistle for Christmas Day. Read Isaiah

53, and consider each verse in the context of the Passion narrative of Good Friday. But sooner or later you are left with just your passage (perhaps a BRF portion) and apart from whatever notes you are using you have to ask yourself, 'What does this say to me?'

How can you start?

If you are dealing with a story, try to picture the scene in your mind's eye. If with a sentence (e.g., 'God so loved the world . . .'), try to re-express what it says in your own words. That will help to clear the meaning in your mind. If with a brief prayer (e.g., 'In thee, O Lord, have I put my trust'), say it several times over, so that it crops up from your subconscious mind during a busy day.

Pray before you read. The old verse from a Psalm will do quite well: 'O Lord open thou mine eyes: that I may behold the wondrous things of thy law'. The Bible not only *was* the word of God; it can be God's living word to you now.

By means of the Bible you can hope with God's ancient people. You can 'touch and handle' the Word made flesh. You can share that life which is 'hid with Christ in God'. You can in heart and mind ascend with Christ, and with him continually dwell. It is the function of the Holy Spirit to take of the things of Christ, and to show them unto you.

I may mention two sources of help, both very old-fashioned, and as some might think, out of date. One is the great commentary of Matthew Henry (1662–1714)[2]. You need leisure (and some money) to get it and study it, but even to dip into it in a library is to see once more that 'the well is deep'. Few commentators have seen as much in Holy Scripture as he saw.

There is one important principle in meditation (a principle of which Matthew Henry is a remarkable exponent) which all can apply in their Bible reading once they catch the idea. The idea might be described as the generalisation of particular statements. This sounds rather a mouthful and perhaps an example might be useful. This particular example does in fact owe something to Matthew Henry but many examples could be given which do not.

If you turn to the first chapter of St John's Gospel you will find (in the Authorised Version) two uses of the phrase 'Come and see'. For convenience take the second one first. It is where Nathanael, having heard from Philip that Philip and his friends had found the Messiah, and that it was Jesus of Nazareth, replies, 'Can any good thing come out of Nazareth?' Philip's reply is, 'Come and see'. Now if this is treated as merely a repetition of a dialogue which happened one day in the first century between two people it is virtually of no importance. Its only significance arises when the underlying principle is detected, and this underlying principle can then be applied to countless other situations. The underlying principle is that Nathanael puts up a totally irrelevant objection to coming into contact with Jesus Christ. He carries with him a prejudice, however arrived at, against the town of Nazareth, and he uses this as a barrier against contact with Jesus. Philip's reply, however, overcomes this barrier. He says, 'Come and see'. In other words he says, 'Lay aside your prejudice. Forget that Jesus is a Nazarene. You may or may not be right in thinking that Nazareth is a poor place from which to find a Saviour. Try it out for yourself. Come and see'. This generalisation having been arrived at it can be applied fruitfully to all the other objections that people raise today and that we may raise in our own minds against some advance in our personal religion. Every clergyman has heard this excuse when he invites people to come to church – 'I used to have to go so much in my childhood that I never want to go again'. There are all kinds of others. For example, 'You don't have to go to church to be a Christian. There are just as many good Christians outside the church as there are in it'. Or again, 'All religions are the same as far as I am concerned. It is only conduct that counts'. So we can go on filling in our own petty excuses and prejudices which may prevent us from taking a step forward in our Christian lives and experience. Against them all Philip's simple word, 'Come and see' is the real answer. We can only discover the truth by experiment. We must lay aside prejudice and enter open-mindedly into opportunities that lie before us.

Now come back to the earlier 'Come and see'. Here we have Jesus, who has been identified as 'the Lamb of God' by John the Baptist, and two disciples (apparently of John the Baptist) follow him. Jesus turns and asks them what they want. To this they reply, 'Master, where are you staying?' Jesus then says to them, 'Come and see'. Here we have a totally different situation. The two followers are not trying to escape from Jesus but trying to get nearer to him. Something about him, or about what John the Baptist has said, makes them eager to learn more, and although they follow discreetly behind Jesus they are clearly anxious to make closer contact with him. To them Jesus makes an immediate response. Finding them following him it is he who takes the initiative and asks them what it is they are requiring. When he knows he does not make any excuses in the way some of us might be tempted to do. He does not say, 'I am tired now. Come another time'. He does not say, 'Wait until I appear in public again'. He allows his own privacy to be invaded and he graciously invites them to discover what they most want to know, namely his temporary dwelling place. They accept his invitation and stay with him for a considerable time.

This incident, even unadorned and unexpanded, clearly has its own message, but when its significance is expanded the message becomes relevant to any reader at any time and in any place. In it we see that our faintest longings for Christ are welcomed by him and encouraged. He takes even the most uninformed curiosity and turns it into something spiritually beneficial. His 'Come and see' is addressed to all men everywhere: 'Come unto me *all* ye that labour and are heavy laden and I will give you rest'.

So these few words 'Come and see' twice repeated stand on the pages of Scripture both as a warning and as an invitation. A warning against trivial objections to religious claims and an encouragement to follow up even our weakest aspirations towards faith and the truth.

It takes a little time to see how individual phrases and incidents can apply over a much wider field than would appear probable. It is however my own experience both in meditation and in preaching that this ability to see the wider implications of the localised events or statements is one of the real secrets of personal appreciation of the truths of Scripture.

Another aid is the little volume called 'Daily Light on the Daily Path'[3]. There are great limits to what that little book can do, but it has a way of turning the words of the Bible into personal prayer and meditation. Do not despise it.

You must not expect every passage of the Bible, even after meditation, to give you 'a thought for the day' there and then. Some passages must be read as background material to help you understand other passages. As an example we could think of Hebrews 11, that great roll-call of those who, in Old Testament times, walked by faith and not by sight. But if we have never heard of Enoch, Abraham, Isaac, Jacob, Moses and all the rest, much of the significance of the Hebrews chapter will be lost on us. For this reason it is wise to read regularly, preferably with an ordered scheme such as that provided by the Bible Reading Fellowship. Sometimes we shall be filling in gaps, building up the background for a biblical view of life. Sometimes we shall come face to face with Christ, and like St Thomas, falteringly say, 'My Lord and my God'.

Above all, never give up. Remember how an unartistic friend of J. M. W. Turner the artist said to him on looking at one of his pictures, 'I never saw a sunset like that'. 'No', said Turner, 'but don't you wish you could?'

Notes

1. Bengel's Latin is so neat as to justify quotation: 'Te totum applica ad textum: rem totam applica ad te'. (R.R.W.)

2. The work, entitled *Exposition of the Old and New Testaments*, was produced in 1708–10. Its great appeal lies, not simply in the beauty of its language and good, sound common sense, but chiefly in its suggestiveness which starts off the reader on his own train of thought. (A two-volume abridgement of the New Testament commentary is now available: *Matthew Henry's Commentary*, Hodder and Stoughton, 1974, 1975.)

3. This volume consists entirely of the words of Scripture but the selection means that a great variety of themes are covered. The selection is anonymous.

Study Projects

Chapter 1   Deep Literary Appeal

1. Some Everyday Usage of Biblical Language
See how many of these phrases you use and whether you can
identify their contexts in the Bible:

> *the fat of the land; smite them hip and thigh; sow the wind and
> reap the whirlwind; play the fool; set your house in order; salt
> of the earth; an eye for an eye; safe and sound; the powers that
> be; the love of money is the root of all evil; old wives' tales;
> fire and brimstone.*

2. A Musical Bible Study
Play a recording of the 'Hallelujah Chorus' from Handel's
Messiah. The words are taken from the book of Revelation.
> *'Hallelujah . . . for the Lord God omnipotent reigneth' (19:6b
> AV); 'The kingdom of this world is become the kingdom of
> our Lord and of his Christ, and he shall reign for ever and
> ever' (11:15b); 'King of Kings and Lord of Lords' (19:16).*

'Hallelujah' (or 'Alleluia' in NEB) means 'praise the Lord'.

The writer of Revelation was using word-pictures to convey his assurance that despite the cruel power of the Roman
emperor Domitian and the fearful persecution of the Christians, the Lord had not forgotten his people. Against all
appearances to the contrary, governments and despots were
in his hands and the last word would be his.

Handel added music to heighten this triumphant assertion.

How would you convey the conviction that 'God rules'
today in spite of many appearances to the contrary?

What 'pictures' in sound, music or art would you choose?

Chapter 2   Deep Mines of History

1. God and his Wonderful Universe

Look up the following passages to see how the ancient peoples visualised the universe and how the biblical writers used these concepts in speaking of God and man's relationship to him.

> *Genesis 1:6–19; Genesis 7:11–14;*
> *Job 22:12–14: Job 26;*
> *Psalm 88:1–6; Isaiah 40:21–23.*

Here is a suggested reconstruction of how the universe may have been conceived:

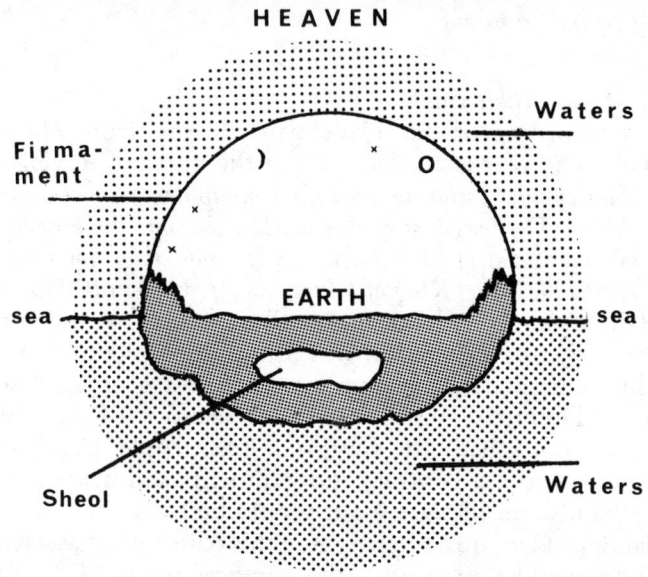

How does our present understanding of the universe affect the ways we think of God, ourselves and our environment?

2. History Repeats Itself

READ ACTS 10 AND 11
Peter felt a deep loyalty to the religious and social institutions in which he had been reared. Yet he also saw Gentiles responding to the gospel and as a chief leader of the young Church he was deeply exercised about how to understand and react to the new situation developing.

What new situations and ideas – moral, religious, political, social – do you feel especially testing in national and church life?

How do you try to distinguish between changes that are wrongly or mistakenly inspired, and those that come from God?

Chapter 3   Deep Personal Piety

1. An Exercise in Spiritual Photography
Using the processes of photography try this meditation on Psalm 23:

> **Focus** *on the key words – 'shepherd'; 'I lack nothing'; 'he shall feed me'; 'green pastures'; 'he shall convert my soul'; 'I will fear no evil'; 'goodness and mercy shall follow me for ever'.*
>
> **Expose** *your mind to the light in these phrases and give thanks.*
>
> **Develop** *these half-understood and half-accepted thoughts in the 'dark room' of your daily life.*

(Based on a paragraph in *About the Bible* by F. W. Moyle, G. Bles 1956.)

2. What is Man?
Who are we; where did we come from; where are we going to? These are questions people have always asked. Today, as man increasingly understands, controls and shapes his environment, and yet cannot always understand or control himself, the question 'What is man?' is more pressing than ever. While many passages speak to this theme let us look particu-

larly at Psalm 8 and see what it says about our human significance in the context of God's glory and the vastness of the universe.

Try to interpret Psalm 8 for today by:
(a) performing it as a mime;
(b) re-writing it using modern images and allusions; setting it in our present-day technological, atomic society.

Also consult these other passages for further insights: Genesis 1:26–28; Hebrews 2:5–11; 1 Corinthians 15:20–28; Luke 9:21–27.

Chapter 4   Deep Memories of the Lord

1. 'The Church's principal link was with the Living Lord' (page 35). The early Christians did not need 'gospels'. They were conscious of the 'living and abiding voice' of the risen and ever-present Saviour. This is well expressed by the saying, 'No apostle ever remembered his Lord'.

How does our having the written gospels affect our links with the Living Lord? Is there too much looking-back in our Christian life?

Does 'an extension of the Incarnation' mean anything to us now? Do we follow Jesus through at least the outline of his earthly days – e.g. in the Christian Year's festivals and special readings?

How should the Easter faith inform and colour our Bible reading?

2. Redaction criticism (page 38) is best met by comparing how the same material appears to have been used in different gospels.

One compares not only the setting but also the exact wording.

examples	Mark	Matthew	Luke	John
Baptism	1:9–11	3:13–17	3:21–22	1:29–34
Temptation	1:12–13	4:1–11	4:1–13	
Sending-out	6:7–13	10:1–11	9:1–5	
Parable		18:10–14	15:3–7	10:1–16
'You are . . .'	8:27–38	16:13–28	9:18–27	6:66–71
Transfig- uration	9:2–8	17:1–8	9:28–36	
Gethsemane	14:32–42	26:36–46	22:40–46	(12:27–30)

Using the clues provided by such comparisons, we can attempt an outline of each gospel. It is significant how much space is given to what.

A book which answers its own question is N. Perrin's *What is Redaction Criticism?* (Fortress Press and SPCK, 1970).

3. Journey to Jerusalem (page 38).

Map and illustrate a modern Christian journey; e.g. with a frieze or a slide-tape presentation, or a scrap-book log. Missionary societies can provide material and parish links supply details. If the situation has involved someone moving into unknown and dangerous territory, so much the better.

How much is a journey (or pilgrimage) still a living image by which we can describe the Christian experience? One of the Church's recent labels is 'the pilgrim Church'.

Chapter 5 Deep Reflections on the Faith

1. Bible Study: hymns in the New Testament letters, using Philippians 2:5–11, 1 Timothy 3:16, Colossians 1:15–20, Ephesians 5:14, (1 Corinthians ch. 13). References to the singing of hymns: Acts 16:25, 1 Corinthians 14:26, Ephesians 5:19, Colossians 3:16; also, the vision of a song-filled heaven in Revelation reflects the practice of the early Church.

Notice the *contexts* of these hymns: they are usually set in very practical, down-to-earth passages. The epistle-writers punch home a message by using a familiar set of words from common worship. High theology and blunt ethics are allied.

What familiar hymns or worship refrains could be used today to similar effect? What hymns (from any period) best express our convictions about who Jesus is, what he has done, what he is doing in the Church?

2. Notice and note down over a period the modern church 'epistles' you receive or hear of – i.e. books, pamphlets, 'open letters', reports, TV programmes, recorded interviews, broadcasts, cassette messages, etc. – especially those by Christian leaders giving guidance on moral issues.

Is their form at all similar to the New Testament epistles? How much gospel and theology is featured? Are the writers/ broadcasters closer to their readers/audience than were Paul, Peter, John or James? What advantages did the New Testament writers have over modern church leaders and their use of our many 'media'?

How much deepening of our vision of Jesus happens? Two books which are relevant: Malachi Martin, *Jesus Now* (a very sophisticated, amusing approach) and David L. Edwards, *Jesus for Modern Man* – both Collins paperbacks.

3. Read an epistle out loud – at one sitting (either as an individual or in a group). Philemon is the shortest and simplest. Galatians is perhaps the most exciting. Romans can be very rewarding when seen as a whole.

Use a modern translation if possible.

Record Ephesians 1:3–14 read from a modern version. Play the recording to a group without any announcement or hint of its origin. (Discover other passages which can make a surprising impact today, if met with fresh minds.)

Chapter 6   Deep Longings for Life Eternal

1. Read 1 Maccabees chs. 1–4, with a commentary if possible; failing a commentary, the Jerusalem Bible is helpful. (In most other Bibles 1/2 Maccabees is in the Apocrypha, between the Testaments.)

Also relevant is Daniel – chs. 2 & 7 (visions of world history coming to a climax with the Jewish struggle against Antiochus Epiphanes) and ch. 6 (a typical 'encouragement story'). Use a commentary with the Daniel passages; e.g. Raymond Hammer's in the Cambridge series.

James Michener's *The Source* (1965: Random House and Secker & Warburg, also Corgi) is a powerful historical novel of the saga variety. It has helped many to appreciate the intense struggles through which the Jews have persevered in faith (and *to* faith, each crisis widening his people's vision of God).

2. 'The real point was, "Is there a resurrection at all?" . . . Christ's answer was profound' (page 59). Read Mark 12:18–27 in the light of its whole context (ch. 12) – mainly controversy about mankind acknowledging God as the source of life.

References to the *Old Testament*: Deuteronomy 25:5 and Exodus 3:6.

See *commentaries*: C. F. D. Moule (Cambridge); D. E. Nineham (Pelican).

Does such Rabbinic argument carry any force today? Should we expect it to? Do we make insincere use of Scripture? How do we think about God only within boundaries pre-set so as to justify ourselves? Whose God is our God?

What can this 'incident' be seen to express about Christian faith and life in the Church?

3. Introduce others to David Winter's *Hereafter* (Hodder paperback). Review it for your local magazines. From its Introduction: 'The time has come, surely, to reinstate the full Christian doctrine of eternal life to the high place it deserves, in our pulpits, on our lips, and in our hearts. This book is simply a provocative attempt to make twentieth-century people look again at something that has meant so much to past generations, and has been needlessly and arbitrarily rejected by the very age that needs it most.'

Very relevant too is the BRF sound-strip 'The Sting of Life', which outlines a positive and Christian attitude to life and all its deaths.

4. Obtain a reproduction of the Van Eyck painting 'The

Adoration of the Lamb' (see page 63). Discover something about the dates and background of the artists. Notice which aspects of their contemporary scene appear in the painting.

What features are most true to the poetic 'vision' in Revelation?

How could a modern artist best treat such a subject?